Helping Students Learn
to Write Poetry

Related Titles of Interest

Helping Students Learn to Write
Joyce C. Bumgardner
ISBN: 0-205-17571-6

Helping Students Learn to Write Poetry

An Idea Book for Poets of All Ages

Joyce C. Bumgardner

Allyn and Bacon
BOSTON   LONDON   TORONTO   SYDNEY   TOKYO   SINGAPORE

Copyright © 1997 by Allyn & Bacon
A Viacom Company
160 Gould Street
Needham Heights, Massachusetts 02194

Internet: www.abacon.com
America Online: keyword: College Online

Limited portions of this book first appeared in *Helping Students Learn to Write* by Joyce C. Bumgardner, copyright © 1996 by Allyn & Bacon. Reprinted/adapted by permission.

Library of Congress Cataloging-in-Publication Data

Bumgardner, Joyce C.
    Helping students learn to write poetry : an idea book for poets of all ages / Joyce C. Bumgardner.
        p.   cm.
    ISBN 0-205-26169-8 (pbk.)
    1. Poetry--Study and teaching. 2. Poetry--Authorship--Study and teaching.   I. Title.
    LB1576.B889   1996
    372.64--dc20
                                                        96-34752
                                                        CIP

Printed in the United States of America
10 9 8 7 6 5 4 3 2 1   01 00 99 98 97 96

Call for a star
Stars in the sky
loving stars
happy stars
dreaming stars
stars to light the sky

in trouble
call for a star
he will calm you down
he will help you.

—Lee Craig, grade 5

To all those students and teachers who, through the marvelous alchemy of
words, have spun their heartsongs into poems,
then shared them with us here—

To famous and not-so-famous poets whose writings have inspired all of us who
learn from them and write poems of our own—

To my cheerleaders, my friends and family, who understand
and celebrate with me when students create poetry—

To the teachers in my life who have helped me to find my own poet's voice—

To K.B., my most favorite poet of all—

My everlasting thanks.

—Joyce Bumgardner

C ONTENTS

Introduction   ix

1. How Does Poetry Begin?   1

2. What's in a Poem?   11

3. First We Listen, Then We Write   23

4. Color Them Real   31

5. Helping Beginners   39

6. Poets Working Together   45

7. Teachers, Let's Talk!   49

8. Poetry Sampler—Poems by Teachers and Students   61

INTRODUCTION

Several years ago, teachers attending my workshops began asking, "Where is the book?"

"What book?" I responded.

"The book about your young poets and their poems," they answered. Finally, here it is.

This book is not about poems that rhyme. It is about helping students sing onto paper those poems that say what is inside them. It is about the innate ability of children to think and feel deeply, to express their thoughts and feelings in the direct and clear way that belongs particularly to them.

Many people have tried to say what a poem is; no one definition is adequate. Webster says it is "an arrangement of words, especially a rhythmical composition, sometimes rhymed, in a style more imaginative than ordinary speech." But poetry is more than that. Even young children can tell us that poetry is a special way of speaking, a way of finding the right words to tell what we feel and know deep inside, and what we have experienced, dream and remember. In a poem we communicate to others our thoughts and feelings through carefully chosen words and phrases.

It has been said that many people "die with their music still in them." Poetry allows us freedom to sing that music onto paper in our own songs—happy songs, sad songs, angry songs, lonely songs, peaceful songs—music from deep inside. Writing poetry, even reading others' poetry that speaks what we feel, gives us a way to sing our songs. Poems sung from the heart move us in a special way, causing a response in the mind and the heart of the reader as well as the writer. In a poem, something is left unsaid, and yet the reader sees, feels, understands and knows what the poet is saying—truly hears the poet's song. Poetry is music to be shared.

Poetry also is like a sculpture made from clay that has been softened and shaped to exactly what the artist wants and needs it to say.

It seldom takes shape quickly—the sculptor must begin working the clay, consider what it will become, then push, pull, stretch and shape it. Like a sculptor, the poet combines the imaginary and the real, puts thoughts on paper in such a way that the words—the symbols—create something real. Following is a poem in which the writer has created real anger on paper—and then, a dissolving of the mad into gentleness.

Water emotions
Black words
lightning across the room,
crash against the wall,
set my hair on fire.
I cartwheel out of there
in a mad red.

Pedaling fast, I'm
a sizzling blur
of tense emotion storming
by;

the soft rain soon
touches fingers of sweet wet
across my back,
melts whatever I'd
been rushing from.

Pace slows,
I drown in giggling children,
sunny gardens,
summer air.

Reading her poem, we feel the poet's *mad red* anger, race with her from the room and angrily pedal into the sweet, wet rain; and we pause, too, to slow, then "drown in giggling children, sunny gardens, summer air." Using strong words, the poet has passed her feelings to us. Poetry communicates in a unique way, makes us feel the poet understands us, says exactly what we might say if only we could find the right words. Writing poetry is the art of making something real, starting with nothing at all but one's thoughts, feelings and words, writing tools and paper. From those ingredients come poems singing so clearly that others can hear them. In poetry, we also look for meaning beyond the words—for what has been left unsaid; we use the poet's words to understand meanings beyond them.

It is difficult to put one's deepest, truest feelings into rhyme and meter. When we need to pour out our feelings, we may feel confined and frustrated if we must fit them into rhyme, pattern, "so many" beats to a line, capitalization and punctuation, all according to rules. Your students may be relieved to learn that rhyming is not required for a poem to be a poem. Most often, it is not in rhymed verse that their poets' voices speak best, but in a free language filled with feeling, with simile and metaphor, and with words that together create the *sound of poetry* and that speak important truths without concern for line length, rhyme or meter. Students who are expected to create lines of "so many" syllables may be able to do so— it's a simple form, after all—but what they write may not be *poetry*.

Krissen had something important to say in "Grandpa," a deeply felt poem comparing her memories of her grandfather to his current state of illness. Imagine what might have happened to the tender feeling in this poem if Krissen had been required to write it in rhyme.

Grandpa
My grandpa has Alzheimer's.
He doesn't understand.
It makes me unhappy
but not mad.

But then I think,
MEMORIES.

When Grandpa would put me on his lap
sing Ride a Cock Horse
and bounce me up and down
I·would listen to his funny jokes
with his twinkle in his eye,
smell the aroma of Grandma's cooking
Grandpa's falling asleep.
Carefully I get off his lap,
quiet not to wake him,
hear his quiet breathing
which gives me no worries, no cares.

Now I look into Grandpa's eyes
Nothing shows he understands
Except the twinkle in his eye.

—Krissen Johnston, grade 6

This book is written to show you how to help yourself and your students acquire a feeling for poetry, a love of poetry, and the ability to write what you and they think, know, feel, want and dream. It isn't hard—most children have an instinctive understanding about the language of poetry. Much of your work as nurturer and as teacher will involve both reading to them and providing for them to read a deep, rich variety of poetry, both rhyming and nonrhyming, of many poets' styles and voices. Help them to fill their minds with sounds of poetry so that when they have important things to say, they will be prepared to write.

There is a wonderful, unique bond experienced by poets who come together to read and to share their poetry. Visit with your students—sometimes alone, sometimes in group settings—about their poetry. Such discussions can help students learn to ask questions, make helpful comments and appreciate each other's writing, creating an atmosphere that allows them freely to write and to share their poems.

Poets know that reading others' poems gets us ready to write and triggers thoughts and ideas for poems of our own. One student's poem can act as jumper cables for another's. The anthology section of this book contains your students' jumper cables—poems written by students to be read and heard by your students as they write poems of their own. Children everywhere share similar thoughts, experiences and understandings; hearing poems written by others like them will prepare your students to begin writing their own. Poems in this book were chosen because they are fine examples of universal truths known and understood by children everywhere; because they have in them their creators' hearts; and because they speak strongly, leaving lasting impressions on those who read them. They may make you laugh, feel deeply, want to dance for joy, or even weep. Some of the poems have within them a mysterious, glowing *something* that makes us wonder how it is that children's voices can speak to us so clearly. These are *their* voices, *children's* voices, singing, dancing, watching, listening, grieving, rejoicing in their own words—*in poetry*. They have discovered poetry to be the right vehicle for their words, for their voices.

Also provided is a section of teachers' poems that will help you start writing poems of your own. Many will make you want to read and think about them again and again. Read these wonderful pieces, and when you are ready to try your own poetry voice, begin.

Poems in this book have been created by teachers and students from all ability levels. No one will know, reading these poems, whether they have been written by more advanced or less able writers; *anyone* may be gifted with the heart and voice of a poet. The poems have been gathered from students and teachers in large city schools of more than a thousand students and from small rural schools where the entire student body from grades kindergarten through six numbers eighty. But each poem shares two things in common: Each speaks with a clear *voice*, and each has been written by a *real poet*.

Years of "talking poetry" with students and teachers have shown me that the language of poems can become, for many children and adults, the best voice and the strongest language they own. It is my hope that reading this book—seeing and hearing what children and adults have spoken with their poets' hearts—will inspire you to write your own poems and to nurture your students as they explore the rich, exciting and satisfying world of poetry.

Every possible effort has been made to identify and obtain permission from teachers and students to use their poems in this book. Many students wrote notes back to me saying, "Please use my name!" In other cases, wonderful poems were given to me by young poets from large writing groups as our time together came to an end; occasionally, no name or only a first name was included on those papers. Perhaps, due to those poems' content, that was done deliberately because the poets wished to remain anonymous. To those unidentified writers, as well as to those whose names I know well, go my warmest thanks. Your poems now go out into the world where others will hear your poets' songs.

Finally, the ideas in this book have been gathered over years of writing with students and teachers. Some have been shared by other teachers as examples of successful poetry-writing efforts in their classrooms. As a classroom teacher myself, I am very aware that few ideas are truly original. We teachers borrow, adapt, share and put our own mark on ideas we see and hear; and success in our own classrooms with those ideas becomes something others want to try too. They, in turn, borrow, adapt and alter the ideas with their own special knowledge—and "original" ideas are born.

To all who have shared with me, thank you. What could be more satisfying than to see others use these ideas successfully for the good of their students and themselves? I am excited about the possibilities presented by the publication of this book and hope it will provide teachers everywhere with new ideas for helping students and themselves to find their voices, their heartsongs.

—*Joyce C. Bumgardner*

1. HOW DOES POETRY BEGIN?

Most of us find our introduction to poetry as babies. We start with nursery rhymes, those bouncy, perfectly rhymed verses we as children loved to hear and say in our sing-song-y voices over and over again. Generations of us have chanted these poems as small children, and, as adults, we can recall one after another, saying them by heart for a lifetime. Hearing and saying nursery rhymes is a wonderful way to begin developing a love of poetry.

"Hickory dickory dock,
The mouse ran up the clock.
The clock struck one
And down he run,
Hickory dickory dock."

A small child skips happily through the house, swinging her head, feet and hands in the pattern of the rhyme, saying it over and over.
My own love of poetry began with Robert Lewis Stevenson's "The Swing."

How do you like to go up in a swing,
Up in the air so blue?
Oh, I do think it the pleasantest thing

Ever a child can do!
Up in the air and over the wall,
Till I can see so wide,
Rivers and trees and cattle and all
Over the countryside—

Till I look down on the garden green,
Down on the roof so brown—
Up in the air I go flying again,
Up in the air and down!

I start my poetry workshops with the reading of this beloved rhyme, and often, reading it to a class of teachers or students, I see them softly saying the words with me, tapping their feet, bouncing to its gentle rhythms as the words first heard long ago return to them. Nursery rhymes and other rhyming poems teach a sense of word play, a sense of "line," a sense of what poetry can be.

After years of hearing, saying and moving to the beat of nursery rhymes, it is natural that when children begin to write their own poems, usually in second or third grade, they try to create what they know—poems that sound like nursery rhymes. They are writing what they have heard. Sometimes their rhyming poems work quite nicely; more often, they collapse under the weight of their creators' efforts.

Witness the descent of the poem "Cats" into the abyss of meaninglessness as a young poet forces it to rhyme:

Cats act crazy
as if you didn't know.
When they're hunting, they crouch really low.
Dogs are cats' enemies, also known as foe.
When cats run, they really go.
Cats have claws on their toes.
Cats are pretty as a rose.
Cats walk around as if they're in a pose.
I'm so sorry, but I really must goes.
I'm starting to slows
With my rhyming.

He finishes writing his poem, and with a puzzled look on his face, comes carrying it to me. "Something is wrong with this," he announces.

"What happened?" I ask.

He smiles grimly. "I got stuck!"

Already trained by years of listening to bouncy, perfectly-metered nursery rhymes, this beginning poet followed the pattern he knew; but he could tell it didn't allow him to say what he wanted to say about cats.

"What did you intend to say?" I ask.

"I like cats," he says. "I like the way they purr, and the way they are so soft, their glowing eyes, and the silent way they walk." He goes on, lyrically describing what he loves about cats.

"Now," I say, "write down what you have said, for that is your poem."

I understood about his poem. This was my own experience too with writing poetry—marking off on my fingers A, B, C, D and on through the alphabet as I searched for words to rhyme with those that had come before, rhyming *everything*, whether or not it made sense or was pleasant to the ear. Often it actually was painful. We all did it: Our poetry was *expected* to rhyme. Unfortunately, many students today tell me that their poetry too is acceptable to their teachers only if it rhymes; one young student who had written a lovely poem found the following notation written across it by her teacher: "This does not rhyme. It is not a poem. F."

It was because of the constant, unvarying compulsion to rhyme that I began to dislike poetry. The poems we read and heard *always* rhymed. They nagged. Perfectly formed, metered and rhymed, they seemed like words locked in a square box. I did not find *feeling* in these poems, so they didn't matter much to me beyond the few I liked, and beyond the fun of saying the nursery rhymes I had learned when I was small. And while "Burma Shave" signs added a note of anticipation as we drove along the highways, watching for the next satisfying, perfectly rhymed and metered line, generally I grew weary of poetry at an early age.

When I was seven, my mother began taking me to visit a marvelous woman named Myrtle Sylvia Johnson. She spent her life in a small room, confined to a wheelchair. Beyond her kindness and cheerful welcome for all who came to visit, she was a *poet*. I will always remember hearing and seeing for the first time a poem that talked to me, that said something true and important: It was her poem about looking out the window, waiting and longing for spring. *I waited just as she did.* The difference was, when spring came, I could run and play outside; she could not, and her words touched me deeply as I pondered her view of spring and compared it to my own. I learned her lovely poem then and have never forgotten it:

Invalid's longing
I am waiting for the springtime,
When tne fruit trees are in bloom,
When I'll see them from my window
And breathe their sweet perfume.

And I'm waiting for the summer
When the air is filled with song,
When the flowers grow profusely
And the days are bright and long.

Oh, I love all nature's seasons—
Each one has its special charms,
But the budding, blooming period
I await with open arms.

I loved Myrtle's poem; it was personal—it was *hers*. It sang her own song of longing, and my poet's heart heard and loved her song. Now, in addition to Robert Louis Stevenson's *The Swing*, I had another poem to love.

Fourth grader Anastasia Krupnik, the main character in Lois Lowry's delightful book of the same name, writes a poem assigned for Creativity Week. While Anastasia creates an intriguing, image-filled poem, the rest of the class and their teacher struggle grimly forward, putting poetry into the only "acceptable" form they know, that of rhyme. And while other students' rather primitive efforts are rewarded with A and B+ grades, Anastasia receives an F, because, as her teacher informs her, her poem does not rhyme. Worse, it has no capital letters or punctuation. Anastasia has not followed directions, says Mrs. Westvessel.

Anastasia goes home, takes out her green notebook and, where she had written earlier "I wrote a wonderful poem," she erases *wonderful* and changes it to *terrible*. "I wrote a terrible poem," she writes sadly.

During my student years, most of the poetry we read and heard was *nice* (a rather innocuous term); most, if not all of it rhymed, and it was tiresome. At the time I didn't know how to put words together to make them rhyme well *and* say anything of importance; thus, poetry wasn't a form of writing or reading I pursued outside the classroom. My personal journal writing seldom involved efforts at writing poetry, though I did win a contest in high school with a rather awful poem that rhymed perfectly.

When I became a teacher and it was time for my class to learn about writing poetry, I introduced the unit by reading aloud the kind of poems I'd heard most often in my own growing years: the rhyming kind. It was all I knew. Naturally, my students' poetry too nearly always rhymed, whether or not it made sense. And often it sounded as if it had been pounded together with hammers as students went back and forth over their fingers seeking words to rhyme with what had gone before. I saw my students' feelings of frustration as they tried to make their poems rhyme. While it can be satisfying to write poetry that rhymes, and many rhyming poems are exactly as they should be, children need to know there can be more to poetry than rhyming, more than form, meter and rules. Too often, rhyme *subtracts from* rather than *adds to* poems, and the content is unimaginative. My students had so much more to say than rhyming allowed them.

As a teacher and sometimes a poet, I was frustrated too. How could I move on to better ways of writing poetry? How could I help my students to do the same?

Meanwhile, our middle child was writing poetry. It seldom rhymed, and it *sang*. I loved her ability to write what was inside her poet's heart. Following examples in books she loved, and under the guidance of teachers who understood and loved poetry of all kinds, she wrote true poems filled with meaning—poems that often made me laugh or brought tears to my eyes, poems that *said* something. I wanted to write poetry like that!

The search for my own language, the language of poetry, had begun. I studied and bought books from local bookstores, camped out in poetry sections in libraries, searched everywhere for *my kind* of poetry. And I soon discovered that by the 1950s many poets had come to see *form* in poetry as repressive and limiting and were writing free verse which, says the outstanding book *Contemporary American Poetry*, was "spontaneous and flexible." They were using poetry to speak of personal, not general feelings, using line lengths determined "by the poet's breathing and fragments that leap kinetically down the page." They began to communicate in their poems much that had not been spoken in poetic form, to make poetry personal in ways not accepted before. They had planted seeds of new poetry that would speak in a real way to many people who, like me, had found little personal meaning in the rhyming poems of childhood.

The more I read, the hungrier I grew for it. Words of other poets began talking to me, often calling forth the *aha!* from my heart. Poems began taking form inside me, wanting to get out onto paper. Now I *had* to write words like this. Often I could literally *see* the lines of words in my mind even before I wrote them down.

I began hesitantly, tentatively to learn the language. My father had died many years before. Every year since his death I had tried to write about him, but each effort ended in frustration, sometimes in tears, with crumpled papers filling the wastebasket. Could poetry help? Sixteen years after my father's untimely death, I was able to write about him in "Magic Hands." In poetry.

Magic hands
When I was small
and Easter took us to the farm
your magic hands turned
brown paper sack and
sweet yellow straw to
strong soaring kite.

Small strips of cloth
made ruffly tail
we ran and
wind took kite to sky
to dip and soar,
to cut through clouds
and nearly pull me
off the ground. I wanted to **be**
kite, carried
free, soaring high—fly, kite, fly!
Yet, close to you
so brown and strong,
my safe Ground,
was my best place to be.
Now I fly
bright-colored,
plastic
manufactured kites,
slick, shiny, perfect,
with children of my own
and dream of you and magic hands
that turned paper sack and straw to
strong and wondrous
flying kite.

I have no magic hands.

My poem said exactly what I wanted and needed to say. Then I wrote a poem to my grandma who had died twenty years earlier.

Poem for my grandma
This is a poem for my grandma who
baked terrible cookies hard as rocks
from old ground-up cookies and new flour and eggs
and this is for the grandma who
sang beside me in church every Sunday but
did all her singing on one note
and this is for the grandma who
wore old-fashioned black shoes and
old-fashioned white shoes and
old-fashioned dresses and
one bright red new coat
and this is for the grandma who scolded Grandpa
for giving me candy from his candy jar
and this is for my grandma who never said
I LOVE YOU to me

And this is for the grandma who got up
before the winter sun to shape tiny meatballs and
to make fattigmand and krumkake
and mashed potatoes and red Jell-o for Christmas,
when we all would gather round her table
to eat and eat and eat and share the love
and this is for the grandma who could
rock and cradle and comfort me better than
anyone else in the whole world

and this is for the grandma who
hid Easter baskets filled with wonderful things
for us all to find in marvelous hiding places but who
never got one herself
and this is for the grandma who listened to all my
problems and angers and fears and never said a
bad word about anyone no matter what

and this is for the grandma whose green eyes I have
and this is for the grandma who had
pain and sadness and griefs in her life
"I just lean on the Lord," she said
when I asked how she got through all of those
terrible things

yes, this is for you and it is from me
because oh, you were the best grandma of all!

Soon I was pouring much of my life into poetry. When the hurts of my childhood came back, I wrote *poetry*. When I wanted to tell my own children how wonderful, how incredible they were, it came to me *in poetry*. I wrote poems for my daughters, for my son, and gave them these gifts on my birthday. My own poetry voice had begun to sing, and I was learning that often the best way of speaking about what mattered to me was *in poetry*.

Why had it taken me this long? Could I have learned these things earlier? Oh, how much I could have written, if only someone had shown me this kind of writing! I wanted *children* to learn this form of poetry *now*—as children, not as frustrated adults—to write poetry that said what they cared about, what they felt deep inside. I began to search for wonderful children's poems that did not rhyme and shared them with students, then encouraged them to write similarly.

I brought my simple poetry unit into classrooms, read poems written by other students to my students and encouraged them to write something "like that." They did, and what has happened and why it has happened has changed my life and has changed my feeling that it's *important* to let children write poetry to we *must* let children write poetry.

Starting with David

One day a fourth-grade class and I had spent time preparing to write poetry and discussing what a poem is. Then they brainstormed, writing down words and ideas that came to them as I read aloud poems written by other students. And finally they chose some of these ideas that appealed to them and began to write poems of their own. As they wrote, I walked about the room, peeking over shoulders to see how the new poets were doing. David's paper caught my attention. Where had such a poem come from?

A dungeon

I'm in a dungeon.
It's dark, slimy.
I'm scared,
there are barred windows,
a high moon,
no food but a
dead rat
I know Death will come,
a guard is on the other side
of the barred door
He has an ax
He said come,
he opened the door and
my Death came!

—David, grade 4

Perhaps he had read of prisoners in other countries, I thought, noting how handsome was this tall child with the kind, gentle face. "Does anyone want to share?" I asked. David's hand went up immediately, and he stood to read his poem. As he read "I know Death will come," his teacher burst into tears and rushed from the room. Her students were alarmed, but I whispered to them not to worry, that she would "be all right."

I glanced from the closing door back to David. "Your poem is special," I said. "Where did you get the idea for it?"

"That's how I live," he said simply. "I live in a bad place, with guns and mean guys who shoot each other—and my dad is a drunk," he added. "He hits us a lot. That's what it's like where I live."

After class, I talked to his teacher, whose eyes were still wet with tears. "Yes, it is the way he lives," she said. "But he's never spoken of it at school—that's why I had to leave," she added. "It's the first time he's ever talked about it." *In a poem.*

In another school, sixth graders were writing poetry. They began coming to the front of the room to share with me what they had written, seeking my approval for their poems. That is an interesting part of writing poetry with students: They come, carrying their poetry pages, to ask, "Is this any good?" The poems were fine. Some had a special quality about them. It was the first time these students had written poetry like this.

A sad-faced girl waited in line with the others. Her manner was dejected, and her eyes avoided mine. She handed me her paper but said nothing. I began reading her poems. There were seven. Suddenly I exclaimed, "These are really *good.*" "No, they're not," she said. "But they *are.* You are a poet!" I answered. Obviously, this student was not accustomed to praise. Again I said, "These are fine poems."

"No, they're not!" she insisted.

"Please listen," I told the class as I began to read three of her poems.

Clothes
My clothes show my feelings:
Bright is for happy,
Dark is for sad.
Today I am wearing black.

I looked at her, startled. She *was* dressed in black. I read on.

Doors
They creak like bones.
It scares me, sometimes,
To think, when I get old,
My bones could creak, too.

Now I had goosebumps.

Holidays
Easter for the Bunny
Christmas for Santa
Thanksgiving for Pilgrims
Halloween for witches and goblins
My birthday—for ME!

Yes! I cheered silently.

"Well, what do you think?" I asked her classmates. "Is this girl a poet?"

"Yes, yes!" shouted her classmates, looking at her in astonishment.

When the class left for lunch, her teacher told me, "You have no idea what happened here today. You couldn't know this, but she is the girl everyone in class picks on—the loneliest child in my room. She is new here and has no friends. This was wonderful for her." I had no idea that I would hear, over and over, in other classrooms, in other schools, those same words: "You have no idea what happened here today...."

Some months later, I was writing poetry with a class of fifth graders.

A girl came quietly to me, carrying her paper. "Is this any good?" she asked.

Sadness
Loneliness has cut me
like a knife
even the clouds
seem to
taunt me
It is like a bad dream
Bright colors
seem dull and drab
as I sink into the
depths of despair

My emotions
make me feel like a
patch of muddy snow
on a clear winter morning
and my
imagination
has long ago vanished

The sound of the
piano
down the hall
only seems to give me a
headache
The moon
is covered by
a veil of deep clouds
as I
slip into a
restless
sleep.

—Emily Mattson, grade 5

"Oh, yes, Emily! It's wonderful! Do you ever feel like this?" I asked.

"Yes," she said. "That's how I feel now. We just moved. I left all my friends behind, and I don't have any friends here."

When I asked for volunteers to share their poems, Emily raised her hand. The class listened. Then we talked about what she had written. No child would stand before new classmates and announce her loneliness; the language of *poetry* allowed her to speak of it.

Three years later I was a guest speaker at a young writers' conference, talking about poetry. As the crowd of students came into my classroom, a tall, beautiful girl came right to the front, sat down and placed a paper carefully at the top corner of her desk where I would be sure to see it—and grinned at me. I stepped to her desk, glanced down at the paper and on it saw the poem and its title: "*Sadness* by Emily." That poem, the first she had written that wasn't expected to rhyme, had become a bond between us—something special had happened, and I was fortunate to have shared it.

In another class, a third grader named Ricky found his poet's voice:

Love notes
Love notes are
sweet and nice
and some girls
put love notes
in boys' mailboxes
they write
I LOVE YOU
boys should
do that
too.

A while ago, as I wrote with a fourth-grade class, I noticed the following poem being written by a sad-looking boy. Every word was misspelled, and I wasn't sure I could read it all, so I asked him to read it to me. It was a poem for his mother:

This is a poem for my mom
who works at Northwest Airlines
and scrubs and scrubs and scrubs
and then comes home and
flops on the couch
and falls asleep and
is still far, far away from me.

His poem spoke volumes, telling something, perhaps, about that downcast face. Clearly, while there are those fortunate students who are able to rhyme poems easily and say important things in that way, there are many more whose poets' voices speak best in poetry that does not rhyme or conform to predetermined line lengths or structures.

2. WHAT'S IN A POEM?

When I go into a classroom to write poetry with students and teachers, I invite students to tell me what they know about poetry. "How is it different from other kinds of writing?" I ask. I write their knowledge on the board, and it almost always includes these pieces of information:

1. Though poetry often rhymes, it is not required that it do so.
We discuss the fact that sometimes poetry seems to rhyme almost by itself, gently and naturally; but it doesn't *have* to rhyme, and often the best poetry doesn't rhyme at all. We still can tell it is poetry because it has a flow, a rhythm, even when it doesn't rhyme. We call this *the sound of poetry*. The more poetry we read, the more we come to know the sound of a poem.

The sound of a poem is different from the sound of an essay or a report. We recognize it as poetry because of the poet's careful choice of words and combinations of words. One student, writing a poem about being angry with his dog early in the morning, went on to speak of their joyful play at the end of the day—"as if there never had been made the morning." *The sound of poetry.* The sound of a poem should be interesting, alive. Most often, these words convey to the reader a sense of feeling as well. *It is most important not that a poem rhyme, but that the poet says what he or she feels inside.*

Broken heart
Sitting here I see
a couple
walking hand in hand,
happy together...
I know them well.
I wish I
could be in
his arms
instead of her but that's
impossible but I can't stop
thinkingthingslike that.

My bubble pops
and I'm back on Earth
free to think those thoughts
in my bubble land but
not here.

—Lacy Marie Jacobson, grade 8

2. Poetry is descriptive.

Poets use adjectives, *describing* words, to paint colors, sizes, shapes and textures. Poets also use these words to speak of sounds, feelings, smells, tastes and thoughts. We can *see*, can *smell* in our imaginations the "hot summer sun wrapping itself around the fragrant red rose." We call this *imagery*. Imagery is a way to paint word pictures in the reader's mind by using sensory words, those related to our senses of sound, sight, smell, taste, and touch. Poets choose adjectives carefully, seeking exactly the right words, the specific words, to create images in the minds of readers and listeners.

A peaceful day
Today is a peaceful day—
fish roaming dark waters,
lakes of sunlight pouring in the window,
deep blue sky where hawks circle
while a small bird builds
its nest of twigs and leaves,
rolling waves topping the shores,
bees gathering nectar for their hives,
flowers bursting with rainbow petals,
clouds an ocean of cotton waves,
and me
staring at the sky
wondering
if I will ever see a day
like this
again.

—Mike Graff, grade 5

Description? As clear as a Monet painting!

3. Poets often use onomatopoeia (words imitating the sound connected with things or actions)—in other words, sound effects.

For example, *Clang, clang, clang!* called the bell. Or *Whoosh, whoosh, whoooooosh!* whispered the wind. Dusty's poem about pop can make you thirsty:

Pop
*pop is cold and
hard in the can
cold so cold
waterdrops
on the side
then whoosh POP the can is
opened
all you hear is
fizzfizzfizz the fizz
of the pop
then gulp gulp gulp
the can is
empty*

—Dusty Heise, grade 6

4. Alliteration (repetition of initial consonant sounds) is often effective in writing poems.

Students love playing with alliteration, and it is often a good way for beginning poets to experiment with words.

Silvery   slippering   grass   no sound
   snakes   through the   make   at all.

5. Poetry is personal.

In class we discuss the fact that sometimes others may not understand the poems we write, may not even like what we write, but that does not make our poems wrong. If a poem says what we truly feel inside, it is important. No one can say of another's poem, "That's *wrong.*" Teachers and other listeners may ask questions, may make suggestions, or may help us look for ways to make a poem clearer or stronger, but what we write from our hearts is ours.

First day of deer season
*It's my first time
hunting for deer
by myself
so I'm sitting in my stand
next to the ash swamp.*

*I hear a noise over my head
it's a squirrel*

*I try to make it shut up
shake the branch and
it runs.*

I've put doe scent on the tree
I hear a crashing coming
I'm so nervous I can barely lift
my gun
I see it!
My gun is
shaking in my hands

It's sniffing the tree
There it is
A ten-pointer
My first deer I ever got
First day of season
First time I have hunted alone!
It was so cool—

My brother didn't get anything.

—Richard McCorison, grade 6

Some students may not care for hunting, but this student wrote what had been exciting and satisfying for him.

In a young writers' workshop, a seventh-grade student showed me her poem. It was funny, original. I liked it but didn't "get" it. She watched me, waiting for my reaction.

"I like it," I said, adding, "but I don't understand it."

She grinned. "That's OK," she announced, then carried her poem proudly back to her desk. Her poem belonged to *her*.

My dad is
weird
and so is
my family
speedy is
fast
but I'm still
not funny.

—Jackie Eckblad, grade 5

6. Poetry usually is shorter than other kinds of writing.

Though some poems are long, most poetry makes its point more quickly than other kinds of writing. For example, asked to write what it means to be truly happy, a student might pen an essay of several pages. However, a clear, deep piece about the meaning of happiness is also contained here in a poem of just twelve lines:

Happiness
Happiness, oh happiness,
How do you come
through my anger?

Happiness, oh, happiness,
How are you

always there?

Oh child, oh child,
I come through anger because
you call me.

Oh child, oh child
I'm always there because
I'm part of you.

—Elyse Tadich, grade 3

7. Poetry has a special look.
Inside its covers, a book of poetry does not look like a science book, a geography book or a math book. It may contain short lines, long lines, patterns of lines, sometimes poems written into special shapes. Sometimes a single word has a line all its own; that gives it special attention, makes it stand out. Varying the use of punctuation and the length of lines can make poems look more interesting. We call this the *look of a poem.* We can play with our poems and make them look any way we choose. The way our poems look as we sing them onto paper is important, and part of the fun of creating a final copy is putting it on the page in the way that seems best for each poem. Poems often seem to want to look a certain way on the page and almost tell us how they should be laid out.

The sea

                                                                up.
                                                     surf's
          is   through   you   saying
The sea bouncing   the   and can people
                    ground   new

—Aleea Dugstad, grade 6

Tell students that the initial writing of a poem may simply go onto a page line after line, almost like writing a paragraph. But once the poem has found its way onto paper, the poet can shape it as he or she wishes, marking slashes where a word needs to be "bumped" down to begin a new line. When the arranging of lines has been completed, the poet will copy the poem over again, giving it the structure he or she wants—the *look of a poem.* This is the first writing of "My Secret Place":

My secret place is somewhere but
I can't tell you. My secret place is so secret
that nobody knows about it.
It is my place to get away from
everything and be alone.
My secret place is...my room.

—Chris Robson, grade 4

In his next step, Chris indicated with slashes where he planned to end one line and begin another:

*My secret place is somewhere/ but
I can't tell you./ My secret place is so secret/
that nobody/ knows about it./
It is my place/ to get away from
everything/ and be alone./
My secret place is.../ my room.*

Here is his final version, which now has the *look* of a poem:

My secret place
*My secret place is somewhere
but I can't tell you.
My secret place is so secret
that nobody
knows about it.
It is my place
to get away from everything
and be alone.
My secret place is...
my room.*

8. We are not required to use sentences when writing poems.
Instead, we use phrases and *essential* words. Poets often leave out *a, and,* and *the,* because a poem can be leaner, tighter and stronger without them.

Butterfly
*Butterfly
golden cream
soft fuzz
butter color
tiger stripes
falls to mossy ground
butterfly
golden cream
wings as big as an
apricot*

—Jessie Vollmer, grade 6

8. We are not required to use capitals or punctuate according to the usual rules when we write poetry.
Upon hearing this news, students often giggle or gasp or sigh with unbelieving relief. For many students, often those for whom writing is difficult, it is like being told they are free to write without constraint what they have been holding inside forever. Add to this new understanding the astounding information, again contrary to the rules, that poetry can begin with the words *but* or *because* or *and,* and some students become almost giddy: Writing poems might actually be fun! In fact, students often become intrigued with the poems and style of e.e. cummings and may attempt to write "like he does—it's neat!" This playing with words can be a great invitation to create poetry.

Bubblegum
you can chew til it's
really soft or
blow a big huge bubble or even
share a piece
with someone
and
chew it til your teeth hurt
I spit mine out the car
window

—Krystal Grandson, grade 5

But
but...our society prohibits it, never can it be
first in a sentence, can't be a main idea, always
there, always meaningless

but...means nothing, a boring word say the rules,
it has no rights

but...what is it for (connects two sentences, say the rules)
but...what is its meaning (nothing, say the rules) not in definition
in soul (soul is not in the mechanics of writing, say the rules)

but to me but is freedom in poetry, used first and often.

—Mitch Bullard, grade 8

10. Poems often include repetition.

Sometimes the first line of a poem is repeated elsewhere in the poem. Maybe the first line is also the last line. Perhaps it is used several times in the body of the poem. Readers begin to anticipate the line's return because a pattern has been created. Repetition can be effective in helping a poem to speak with a strong *voice*.

Stop.Listen.
Stop.
Listen.
Do you hear?
Do you see?
Fighting,
hatred,
prejudice.
Stop.
Listen.
Help!
The hurt
the lonely
the hungry
Stop.
Listen.
Just for awhile.   —Erin Adrian, grade 6

11. Poems convey feeling, often strong feeling.

A poem may speak of happiness or sadness, anger or pain, fear or joy, or sometimes two seemingly opposite emotions. Reading a sad poem may make the reader feel melancholy; a happy poem may cheer the reader. I often share these poems about feeling with classes of young writers.

I feel like I'm blowing up!
There's dynamite in my head
exploding and crashing all around.
I run to my room,
slam the door
turn off the lights;

and in my dark room,
the explosion dies down.

"What feeling is expressed in this poem?" I ask. Students understand: Anger. The poet doesn't say *I'm angry*. She shows it with the words she chooses.

When you're afraid,
Your hands get watery.
You feel cold all over
and you want to hold on to something.
Your breathing changes and
Your heart bangs in your ears.
Your stomach jumps around.
It's like being in a dark, dark closet.

"What feeling is expressed in this poem?" I ask. They recognize the fear that permeates the poem.

Neither of the poems rhymes, but they express strong feelings, as poems do, and they carry the sound of poetry—words used in unique, sometimes startling ways, with combinations of just "the right" words. Sometimes poets write angry poems. One student wrote a poem to her father to express the anger she felt at his walking out on her family when she was small. At other times poets write happy, joy-filled poems that nearly sing themselves off the page. One of my all-time favorite joyful poems in all the world is this one, written by a fifth grader who went on and on, rejoicing in spring. His poem makes me happy too!

Spring
spring
what a wonderful thing
when puddles lead to
streams of water
and joy bursts
from dull and boring winter
when flowers bloom
and I smell the sweet
fragrance of spring
and everything is
green and lovely

your heart
is overflowing
with joy
and peace
you roll in the grass
with a friend
and dream
a dream that
can
happen
that's why I love
spring.
O
can there be
anything
better than spring
when rain
sprinkles on you
and you dance
and trees grow
and you climb
and reach
the sky!

—Josh Kleeberger, grade 5

Sometimes poems are sad, mysterious or secretive. Sometimes they speak of worry, sometimes of loneliness. Children often write poems about feeling lonely; everyone has times of feeling lonely, and the writing of poems can become a way to voice those deep, sad feelings.

In one class a boy commented softly, "I read 'My Friend' by Langston Hughes. It's about his friend dying, and my friend died too. Langston Hughes said just what I felt." How exciting to find children making connections with Langston Hughes!

Another young poet's forever friend moved away.

The summer he left me
My friend and I were friends forever until
he left.
I was happy all my summers but one.
I remember hiding from people
in the big dipper on my
8-shaped block.
I remember the smell of summer that
wasn't even a smell.

I remember the sound of summer that
wasn't even a sound.
I remember when we used to talk about
what we were going to do
the next day.

I remember going to school and talking about
how our sisters are weird.

I remember me sitting alone and
my friend coming to get me out of
boring.
I remember him coming to my house
to play that's when he told me he was
leaving
I was
shattered.
He was leaving our place on
the earth
that was only a speck
on the
map.

—Sean Molin, grade 5

12. Poets use just the right words and leave out all the others.
Writing a poem is like creating a sculpture. Talk with students about how they work a chunk of clay. Two or three pats on that new clay do not create a work of art. A sculptor must work the clay, soften it before beginning to push, pull, stretch and mold it into what it will eventually become. So it is with a poem: We begin thinking, then writing the words onto paper just as they come into our heads. Then the real work begins as we smooth, take away what is not needed, select just the right words and work to make the poem exactly as it must be. Rarely is a poem finished after its first writing. Rather, it is as though a poem's rough draft is the clay, now warmed and ready to shape.

13. A good poem contains strong words.
As students work with their rough drafts, they should thoughtfully consider the words in their poems. Are they strong words? *I go across the room* is wishy-washy. How do you *go*? Strong words make movement come alive. Change *go* to *hop* or *slink* or *leap* or *slide*. Adverbs are often unnecessary when sharp, active verbs are used. In the same way, describing words can add life to a poem's imagery: A *good* cookie can be *tummy-pleasing, chocolate-studded, golden-crunchy.* Poets must use vivid adjectives and lively verbs. Poetry is a place for *extraordinary* words!

As students read their poems aloud to themselves they should examine each word to see if it is generic and can be replaced by a stronger word. Such words as *good, nice, very* and *pretty* say little. What is *nice*? What is *good*? Describe what *nice* is (*my friend's hand holding mine*, perhaps, or *like soft, puffy marshmallows*); paint a picture of what is *good* (*the juicy-apple gum flavor*); give an example of what is *beautiful.* Use specific nouns whenever possible.

14. Sometimes a poem seems to have been waiting inside a poet and almost writes itself.
Poetry can come to us so quickly that our writing hands can scarcely keep up. I have a passion for gardening and often have wondered where that love of earth and plants began. Some time ago I was digging in my flower garden. Suddenly, with my hands covered in dirt and my legs stiff from kneeling on the rough soil, I *knew*: I jumped up, hurried into the house, grabbed my clipboard and pencil and ran outdoors again to my swing, where the poem leapt onto the paper.

Hands
*Today I
know why I like to
dig in the dirt
turn over the black earth smell
and rake it smooth—it's
because all the while I'm digging I
feel your strong brown hands
on my small ones as you
show me
how*

—May 3, 1994

The day my poem "arrived"? Twenty-five years to the day after the death of my father, my gardening teacher. And yes, I do talk with students about the "muse," that wonderful, mysterious spirit of inspiration that can appear, seemingly out of nowhere, to give us poems! Often heads will nod in agreement—many of these youngsters have experienced and understand the concept of the muse for themselves already!

15. Poets use figurative language

Poets compare things. Often these comparisons take the form of similes (I feel *as* cold *as* an icicle or I feel *like* an icicle) and metaphors (I *am* an icicle), words that go beyond their literal meanings. Figurative language adds power and life to poems, combining words in unexpected, original and memorable new ways. Ask your students to listen to the following poems, then discuss the similes (comparisons using *like* or *as*) and metaphors (comparisons that do not use *like* or *as*) used in each.

Happy
*When I am happy or
excited I feel like a
balloon with too much air
about to burst*

*When I am happy
filled with joy
I'm the sun that
brightens the day*

*When I am happy
feeling good
I'm a blanket to
warm cold feelings*

*But when I am sad
filled with sorrow
it is a whole different
story.*

*—*Jessica Brannan, grade 6

Skateboarding
Skateboarding
is
rolling thunder
coming down the
sidewalk.

—Chase Anderson, grade 6, *Prairie Winds*, Rapid City, South Dakota

After doing the previous exercise, ask students to look for original similes in their reading and to create their own. "As quiet as a mouse" is old and worn. "As happy as a lark" was used generations ago. Encourage students to use the great creativity and unique thoughts they have inside them to create their own fresh and surprising similes.

16. Personification is used in writing poems

Personification gives human characteristics to such nonhuman things as objects, animals or ideas. Personification becomes metaphor because it indicates that a nonhuman thing is human. One young poet used personification to write of her wonderful feelings of spring:

the sun pushing up against my skin
massaging it like the
warm, kind hands of my dad

17. Often the *punch* or *power* of a poem is found in the last line of a poem.

Fun and excitement
I like fun and excitement
I like to go on roller coasters
screaming
  My stomach is tying itself in tiny knots
    My hands hold tight on the bar in front of me
Twirling
  Twisting
    I feel
excited like I'm going to
  explode or fall off
Corkscrew
  Tunnels
I hear thousands of people screaming
      I see them lifting their hands
  Sick
  Excited
I love this!

—AnnaMaria Sjol, grade 6

Tell your students that, as AnnaMaria discovered in her "Fun and excitement" poem, playing with poetry can be fun! Remind them that they can write poems about anything and everything that matters to them.

3. First we listen, then we write

"How do you teach kids to write poetry like that—poems that don't depend on rhyming or 'so many' lines or syllables?" teachers often ask as they hear the wonderful poems students have written.

The answer is, I don't teach them. I invite them into the world of poetry, reading to them several poems at a time, all written by students like themselves. It is important that they know these wonderful poems are created by writers like them who understand what it is like to be their age, with concerns and problems like their own. Students listen and take notes, brainstorming as they prepare to write. I assure them that they can't do it wrong, that whatever they write will be fine; they need permission to experiment with this new form of writing. Grades are not an issue here; I *do not* grade their poems.

Setting the stage: Getting started

I ask students to take out several clean sheets of paper and a sharp pencil or a pen, then instruct them to listen as I read, jotting down whatever comes into their minds. It might be a word or words right from the poem, or it might be totally unrelated. It doesn't matter: listening to poetry gets our "creative" juices, the right brain, working.

23

For example, while they listen to a poem about winter, one student's brain might say *bubblegum*. That student writes *bubblegum*. Others might write *snowflakes, wind, blizzard, birds* or *skiing*. We make word lists from the top of the page to the bottom like a grocery list, then begin again at the top or on another side. They are not to write a whole poem, only words or short phrases at this point. One poem might suggest several words to them, another only one. I read them a poem like the following:

Small town
Sitting in my grandpa's old truck
in front of the gas station, watching
old men in overalls going in and out
of the gas station, talking about
farms and tractors, drinking pop
that's almost gone, driving off in
old pick-up trucks, going home to
their farms where the cows need to be
fed and the old tractors are falling apart.

—Jeff Gengler, grade 5 *Prairie Winds, Rapid City, South Dakota*

Students begin brainstorming, writing down words that come to mind. Some of their words might be:

truck
gas station
old men
farms
cookies
orange
cows

After reading the poem, and after they have had a minute or two to finish writing, I ask, "What did you jot down?" Several students will volunteer their words, and all will see that while some may have written down a few identical words or phrases, many different words are on paper, some of them are really "far out" (imagination and right-brain creativity at work!), and all of them are acceptable.

I read another poem and another, instructing students to continue jotting down words that come to mind. Often they enjoy hearing the poems so much they need frequent reminders to continue writing—they just sit, listening and enjoying the sounds of poetry!

After reading a variety of ten or twelve poems, including some with "surprise" last lines and some with metaphors and similes that we may stop briefly to discuss, students should have a page filled with ideas.

I tell them to look over their jottings and circle three words that might be fun to turn into poems. Each is a potential poem; they do not combine the words into one poem. Usually several of their ideas have special appeal; those are the ones students choose first.

A far-away place
Next I instruct them to select just one of those three words or phrases and to begin "playing" with it—turning it into a poem. "Do you ever

get so deeply into a book when you are reading that you don't hear anything going on around you?" I ask. Hands go up—children know what it means to be pulled into a good book. "The same thing can happen when you write," I say. "You get so involved in your own writing that you don't even know anyone else is around. I call that 'going into my own far-away place.' If all of us are in far-away places, no one will be visiting with anyone else. This part of the writing we do alone. Later we'll talk about our poems." Then I share with them my observation that we need *time* and *quiet* to create meaningful poetry. Students are given a brief opportunity to ask questions, then are instructed to go into their own far-away places.

Usually someone asks, "How long should my poem be?" The answer, of course, is, "As long as it needs to be to say what you want to say." Usually the poems themselves let students know how long they need to be.

If they have questions, they can raise their hands and I will come to their desks and talk quietly with them. They do not leave their seats; we want to create a thoughtful, quiet atmosphere that will allow them to write meaningful poems. They can write one poem, then another, trying several ideas to see which works best.

The poems begin

Now students begin to write. As they do, I walk around, looking over their shoulders to see that everyone is writing comfortably. "I'm getting ready to write," a student may comment. Or, "I'm thinking." I understand. I need time to begin writing my poems too.

Students must listen to their poems

When several students appear to be finished with a poem, I suggest, "Cover your ears with your hands and read your poems aloud softly to yourself. Your ears will help you to know how your poem sounds. Listen to it. Be an audience. How does it sound?" Students may giggle and feel silly about reading aloud to themselves. You might tell all of them to do this together, instructing, "One, two, three—cover your ears and read." Explain to students that as all of them are reading with their ears covered, listening only to themselves, no one needs to feel embarrassed. Emphasize the importance of writers becoming their own first audience, of listening to the sound of their poems and their voices.

As I continue to walk around the room, observing students writing and listening to their poems, I watch for a poem I can borrow to put on the board, a poem that can be used to demonstrate the technique for giving it the *look* of a poem. Students rarely decline such an invitation.

Working together

While students continue to write, I put the poem on the board just as the student has written it. When most students appear to have completed a first poem, we stop and talk about how we can give the poem on the board *the look of a poem*. Together we decide where to begin and end lines; I use slashes to indicate where words and lines will be moved. Students are encouraged to do the same with their own finished poems.

We may note where words like *a, and* and *the* might be omitted, where words that aren't essential to the poem can be deleted; together we work to give the poem an effective "flow." The poem's creator always has the final decision in making changes. Point out to students how moving a word or words from one line to the next can "pull" the reader along, smoothing the movement of the poem as it is read aloud. In a story, this might be considered using "run-ons"; in poetry, the laying down of lines that end without a speech pause, moving right into the next line, is called *enjambment*.

Canoe trip
The water is calm
the air cool
I'm in a canoe
ahead—small rapids
rushing faster faster we're
tipping over I'm
soaking wet
coming out of the
river's mouth it's
wavy I nearly tip
again I
reach shore
my hands
blistered
I LOVE CAMP!

—Matthew Sager, grade 6

The way a poem is laid out on the page—the visual effect—will indicate much about how it will be read aloud. White spaces, drops from one line to another, the placement of words—all help to give a poem its own special voice. A poem laid out in a long, slim line might indicate a hurrying through mental images and memories, or it might indicate a slowing, a deliberate consideration of each word. The words and the look of the poem will help readers understand the poet's intent.

Sharing their poems
It is important for students to share their poems. Many will be eager to read to the entire class. Others will enjoy sharing in smaller groups or with partners. Remind students of their experiences in learning to read aloud as first graders, when teachers would tell them to "Read with *expression*" or "Read with *feeling*." Encourage them to do the same with their poems, using their voices to convey the feelings expressed in their poems. Poems are meant to be read aloud, perhaps students' own poems most of all.

Reading poetry aloud should be enjoyable, and varying the sound of their voices to match the tone conveyed in their poems—can help make it a positive experience. Invite the entire class to read aloud together the poem you have written on the board. When students practice reading together "with expression," they will be more comfortable reading their own poems without feeling self-conscious. Most students will enjoy doing this. I used to be hesitant about reading my own writing to others, but when opportunities began to present themselves for reading my poetry to audiences, I discovered how satisfying it was. Now my writing of poetry almost *requires* that it be heard by a receptive audience of encouragers! Some students may delight in "hamming it up" as they read.

Students may have suggestions or questions about poems written by classmates or by themselves. Work to create a classroom atmosphere where students feel comfortable discussing what they write and share, a place where their pieces are accepted and praised, where they can find help when they need it, from you and from their peers. Students will be surprised at what their classmates write. They also may be surprised at how others are able to help them write their poems. They may see one another in new ways as they share.

Make sharing easy!

You might want to invite students to push back their desks and come to a corner or to the front of the room to share their poems. Sometimes reading from desks can seem stiff and uncomfortable, while gathering closely together lends a more congenial atmosphere.

As poems are read aloud, some students may discover that their poems were finished before they stopped writing—a last line or two may sound "tacked on." The poem can be written on the board with and without the lines that sound superfluous, and consideration can be given to whether such lines or words should be deleted. The sharing of poems is an opportunity for all students to help one another, the goal being that each writer will have high-quality, important poems to keep at the end of the poetry project or school year. Be sure you share your poems too; you are an important part of this adventure!

Some students may prefer sharing in small groups; allow for this kind of sharing. It may be helpful sometimes to break up into groups of three—two as audience, one as reader/poet.

Continue to assure students that the poems they write will be fine. Tell them, "You can't do it wrong. They are *your* poems, and they will be *right*. No one can say, 'Your poem is wrong,' because it will be *right*." Most students (and many of us) are just beginning poets, fragile, tentative, curious, perhaps reluctant, or maybe even eager to try this kind of writing. We must create an atmosphere where all feel safe using their poets' voices. We have in our classes students who will write poems that soar, poems that weep, poems that say important things in new and unique ways. What beginning poets need from us is thoughtful respect and permission to play with words, permission to write awful and great poems, permission to try this new kind of language...and a role model who also does those things.

Remind students to think: "Does my poem say what I intend to say?" If not, they may need to polish it some more. Changes are allowed.

At the end of writing and sharing sessions ask your students, "Are you pleased with your poems?" Students often are hard on themselves, and feel it might be bragging to say "Yes, I like my poem." Tell them it is perfectly all right to like their poems, that after all the work they have expended on the creating, shaping, refining of their poems, they have every right to be pleased, to be proud of what they have written. That is not bragging.

"Is it any good?"

Students will ask you constantly about their poems, more than any other writing they do: "Is it any good?" The answer must be a question. "Do *you* like it? Why did you write this particular poem? Does it say what you intended to say?" It is important that the poet make that judgment. We all like some poems and do not care for others. That does not mean a poem is not good. A poem's "goodness" is a matter of preference, of one's understanding of what the poet is saying.

Encourage students to collect poems they like, to read all kinds of poetry, and in this way to learn what they themselves consider to be "good." Encourage them to know that we do not write poetry merely "to express ourselves" but that there is purpose in poetry: to communicate with others, to say what is true and important. Often students will model their own poems after the kind of poems they like, and the more they read and write poetry, the more they will learn about their own poets' voices.

While young poets may be thrilled by what they write, as they grow older they may become self-critical, assuming that "adult" poems are better than what they write.

Tell students that their poems are as important, as filled with meaning as any adult poems. I myself usually prefer reading children's forthright poems more than those written by often despairing, cynical, angry adults, however famous they may be, and I tell student writers this. The fact that a poem has been printed in a book does not necessarily mean it is a poem everyone will like.

Tell students that often it is helpful to put away one's poem for a day or two, then take it out and read it again as if for the first time. Needed changes and revisions may be clearly seen during "fresh" readings. Encourage students to read others' poems in books and magazines, to watch, to listen, to observe things closely—to wait. Help them get ready for poems to come.

My third-grade writing-class students were creating animal stories. Katie finished hers and came to ask what to write next. "I don't want to start another story," she said. I suggested that she try some poetry. "I've never written a poem," she answered. "I don't know how."

I handed her a poetry book, suggesting that she might find some ideas in it, and added that often I get ready to write poetry by reading some poems first. She went to her desk, read awhile, then came back. "No ideas, nothing," she said.

"Let's go look out the window," I coaxed. The season was late March, the day gray and ugly like the dirty old winter snow outside. We were all tired of winter, eager for spring to come. We stood by the window, grumbling about the long winter, the dirty snow, the bare trees. Suddenly, Katie announced, "I've got one!" She hurried to her desk, wrote passionately for perhaps ten minutes, writing, crossing out, writing some more. Then she came hurrying to me. "Is this a poem?" she asked.

To Winter
Leave!
Go away!
I'm ready for spring!
I want to see flowers
And hear birds sing.
I want to go swimming in the lake.
I want to ride my bike.
I want to go camping and
Listen to the night and

The leaves blow
And sing me to sleep just
Dreaming of snow.

—Katie Powers, grade 3

Was it a poem? Katie could see from the happy look in my face, could hear in my voice—and her own excitement told her—that it was indeed *poetry*. We hurried to the office and made copies—one each for her teacher, the principal, the librarian, her grandmas, her parents, me and a few extras. The school bell rang, and off she went to celebrate becoming a *poet*.

I saw Katie a week later in the hallway, where she excitedly told me, "I've written a new poem every day since that first one!"

A month later she came to my room to exult, "I'm still writing a new poem every day!" Katie had discovered her poet's voice. And the sharing of her poems was an important part of celebrating that marvelous discovery.

Save them!

Young poets often want to exchange copies of poems. You too may want copies. Insist that students keep one copy of each poem, preferably the original, and make copies to give away. These are important writings, and while students may not understand their significance at the time, weeks, months and years from now many of their poems will come to have great meaning for them. If their only copy is gone, they will never be able to rewrite it in the same way.

Encourage students to save their poems in a portfolio, box or envelope. Indicate that they might want to make changes in their poems at a later time. I show students my own poetry portfolio, crammed with poems. Some are nearly finished, some just beginning, others in the middle of their creation. There is always room for more poems. Teachers should keep folders of their own poetry as well; this modeling is an important part of what we do with students. Don't underestimate the value of your own poetry. You will surprise and please yourself with what you write, and writing your own poems will make you aware of what your students experience as they create.

Your class may choose to compile a poetry book, including poems by every student in your class. A copy should be printed for each student. When the book is finished, your class might read it together, discussing lines that stand out, even choosing some lines as models for new poems. What do they notice about the poems? Their imagery? Their appearance on a page? Word combinations? Originality? Topic choice? New, interesting similes? Metaphors? Sometimes metaphors are so well hidden that the students will have to hunt hard for them. Such discussions at this point should emphasize positive things about the poems. These poems are finished, not works-in-progress.

No grades for poems

How do we grade students' poetry? We don't. What grade can measure the value of a poem from one's heart? No grade can relate to poems like these:

Death
Death
is dreadful.
It can happen to
any living thing.
My grandmother
died
like a snap
like a bullet from a gun.
Now I sing this song
to you
in poetry.

—Rachel Lemon, grade 3

Lonely
When I'm lonely
I feel like
I'm in a dark place and
no one cares.
I feel water
down my face.
My stomach feels like it's on a
roller coaster.
I feel like I'm on a racetrack
racing to get to
happiness.

—Brittney Schwager, grade 3

We nurture our beginning poets and hope that perhaps in writing poems they will find their powerful voices. Writing poetry can set free their imaginations and allow them to say what is in their hearts.

4. COLOR THEM REAL

Tell your student poets:

Listen when words talk to you. Take time to listen, to think. As you begin writing poetry, others may suggest things for you to write about, but, more and more, you will come to know for yourself what you want and need to write.

Keep gathering ideas, keep lists, buy a poetry notebook. Jot down word combinations that come to you. When you are ready to write, use them in your poems. Sometimes you will hear and see entire lines of poetry in your head; write them down, saving them for poems when you are ready to write.

Visit the poetry section of your library. Find poems you like, poems that seem to have been written especially for you. Copy down those you like best. Keep a notebook filled with ideas that come to you as you read others' poetry. Collect poems you love. Buy poetry books for yourself. Then, just as painters try to paint like the "masters," begin writing the kind of poems you like best.

Keep your eyes open: Watch. Listen. Smell. Taste. Feel. Think. Poets must be attentive listeners, keen observers. Above all, *write.* The more poems you write, the stronger your poet's voice will become, and the more poetry you will discover within yourself.

Moving away from rhyme

Sometimes it's hard for students to free themselves from the nursery-rhyme kinds of poetry; they seem compelled to rhyme everything. What do you do then? You might do as I did with one writing student who rhymed all her poems. Her poems never became what she intended, because her head kept forcing her to rhyme:

I like to look inside a book
to see what it might say,
waiting there for me to read
every single day.

"I can't stop rhyming!" she announced in frustration.

Working together, we crossed out all the rhyming words in three of her poems that seemed to have potential. Her challenge was to replace those words with words that said something clearly and succinctly. What a change! As she left rhyme behind, she rearranged the other words as well, until they said precisely what was in her head. Her rhyming poem about reading, which had merely chattered before, now said exactly what she intended:

I enter
a book
when I
open
the cover.
The poems
sit sleeping
until I
awaken them.

Each of her other poems came to life as she learned to let go of the restricting rhyme.

Another way to encourage beginning poets to write without rhyming is to help them write a "guided" poem. Tell them that each line of the poem will begin with the words *I am.* They are to write something to fit each category you name.

1. I am something small that is not alive.
This first line could be: *I am a pebble in the fish bowl. I see everything.*

2. I am something you might find in a garden.
This line might be: *I am a green hoppy frog exploring the garden forest of vines and stalks.*

3. I am something to wear.
I am a soft, silky sweater worn on a cold winter day.

4. I am something used for celebrating.
I am blazing Fourth of July sparklers and Roman candles rocketing into the sky.

5. I am a kind of weather.

6. I am an animal or living creature.

7. I am something that moves that cannot be seen.

8. I am something that makes music.

9. I am something big and strong.

10. I am something soft and gentle.

Students enjoy this poetry project and may want to create their own categories. "Can I do one?" asked an eager second grader.

"You certainly may," I answered.

She responded, "I am something that is sticky." Other students added such categories as something furry, something to be opened, something with a label on it, something in the refrigerator, and something in a forest.

Students who follow these helping ideas are so busy creating original, descriptive lines that they let go of the rhyming. Young children generally will write simply, using perhaps just one describing word. More experienced writers will use several words.

These poems can be meaningful and fun even for adult writers, as in the poem of a young male teacher whose last two lines (I am something big and strong, and I am something soft and gentle) spoke volumes:

I am a dad.
I am a dad.

This poem form can work well as a Mother's Day or Father's Day poem, beginning each line with, "My mother is...." "My father is...." It also can be written using "*You are...*" rather than *I am*.

Remember: Encourage students to write specific, not "generic" poems.

A poem about *a river* comes alive when it is about the Mississippi River. A poem about *pets* takes on life when it is about one's own long-haired, pug-nosed, snuggly puppy. *Love* as a poem topic can be vacuous; love for one's beloved grandmother can become real when it is described with words from the heart.

Poems in living color

What are your favorite colors? What comes in those colors?

Today I am green,
green soft grass,
green growing ivy
green Spanish olives,
green, green, alive!

Yesterday I was yellow,
yellow striped bananas
yellow frosted cupcakes,
yellow garden peppers,
yellow, yellow sunshine.

Tomorrow I will be white,
white crisp daisies,
white linen napkins,
white whipped potatoes,
white, white clouds.

But always I will be purple,
purple, shiny eggplant,
purple silk flowers,
purple, purple ribbons,
purple purple elegance.

Poems created from ordinary, everyday things

Ordinary things lend themselves easily to poetry ideas. As a class, brainstorm a list of ordinary things, putting them on the board as you work together. Your list might include such things as:

ships	swings	animals	birds
fields	rain	sun	moon
stars	trains	flowers	friends
sports	Earth	trees	school
home	doors	windows	chairs
seasons	porches	sidewalks	dreams

Students can use this list, choosing one of these words with which to begin. It is easier for students to start once they have something down on paper, even something as simple as a word from an idea list.

A poem for something or someone

When it speaks of what is good about something or someone, it can be called a praise poem.

Me
Florida has oranges
California has trees
Wisconsin has dairy—
But Minnesota has me!

—Stephanie Andreson, grade 8

Dedication poems

A poem might be dedicated to a favorite person, or pet, or object. For example, the first line might be: *This is a poem for the sky* (for the sun, for the ocean, for my bed, and so on). Or, *this is a poem for my dad* (sister, cat, puppy, and so on).

Poem for my cat
This is a poem for my cat
with your soft white fur
your green glowing eyes
your long tail that sweeps
from side to side.
This is a poem for your
happy meows

for your soft snuggling
while I read.
This is to tell you that you
make me feel
like purring too.

Often a child will write a poem for a grandparent, a favorite aunt or uncle, a special friend. What treasured gifts these make! We live in a time when even children feel they must spend money for presents. We can tell them that they can give a one-of-a-kind gift, a poem written just for that special someone. No one else can give that present.

Be prepared to be surprised
In one classroom, a child wrote a poem about his grandfather who had just died. He was eager to share and read to his classmates his poem that said exactly what he wanted to say about his grandfather.

After he finished reading his poem another student asked in surprise, "Can we really write poems for people who are dead?" Assured that they certainly could, he announced firmly, "Then I will write a poem for my dead sister."

"What will you say to her?" I asked.

"She died before she was born. I will tell her how much I miss her and that I wish she were here, because I never got to have a sister," he said softly. And in his poem, that is exactly what he wrote as other students, inspired by the first two, began to follow their lead. They wrote to people in their lives who had died —to grandparents, to aunts and uncles, to parents, to friends. It became a unique way of remembering these individuals. Many of the students took their poems home to share with family members who, they knew, would understand them. Some would go in the mail to widowed grandparents, aunts or uncles. We made copies of their poems so students would be sure to have one of their own. Again, insist that students keep one copy for their poetry portfolios. They should never give away their only copy.

On your behalf poems
Another first line for a poem is *And I speak for the trees* (mountains, oceans, animals, etc.). We prepare for this kind of poem by thinking, talking about what a tree, an eagle, or a mountain might say to us.

First-line, last-line poems
Some students may find it helpful to begin by writing the poem topic as the first line, then writing words related to that topic below it, ending with a repeat of the first line.

Basketball
running
dribbling
jumping
shouting
bumping
pounding
sweating
shooting
BASKETBALL!

This is not great poetry, but it sometimes works when other ideas do not, and it may lead to the writing of better poems. *It is a way to begin.*

The more poems they write, the more ideas students will have for other poems. Soon they will have a small collection of poems. This is a good time to introduce the idea of keeping a poetry portfolio. This can be a large envelope, a pocket folder, a box—whatever the teacher or student prefers. Students will be proud of their poem collections as they read page after page of their own unique creations. They also will learn that they can have several poems in progress at once, keeping in their portfolios one section for poems-in-progress, another section for ideas and another for completed poems.

Students will learn through experience that the poem they thought was finished one day needs revision the next. They will see that poems need sculpting, shaping, stretching, trimming, polishing until they say exactly what the poets mean to say. It has been said that a poem is never finished. Poets sometimes revise poems even one or more years after they write them. Other times, poems may be nearly complete at the end of the first writing.

As a student writes, reads aloud, and shares his or her poems with others, he or she will develop a poet's ear for what sounds right, a poet's eye for what looks like a poem, and a poet's understanding of when a poem says exactly what is intended.

Skiing
The thought of
skiing
down a hill
on two
polished fiberglass skis
sends thrills
through
my body.

Skiing is an
adventure
full of
daring stunts and
breathtaking jumps
that's what
skiing is.

—Brett Hunek, grade 5

A few words about rhyming
Sometimes poems rhyme so effortlessly we hardly notice it; that is perhaps the best way to write rhyming poetry. Meredith's wonderful poem sings so lightly, so gently that we hardly notice that it rhymes.

Sing
Sing of rain
And butterflies' wings.
Think of everything that
Sings.

Think of the voice
Of the fifth grade choir
As the off-tune notes
Climb higher and higher.
Think of crickets
With whispering wings;
Oh, isn't it peaceful
To think of what sings!

—Meredith Reiches, grade 5

Spring fever
Is is robin o'clock?
Is it five after wing?
Is it quarter to leaf?
Is it nearly time for spring?

Is it grass to eleven?
Is it flower to eight?
Is it half-past snowflake?
Do we still have to wait?

—Jake Nieland, grade 6

Could Jake's poem have been written any other way? Hardly!

More beginnings
To help students get started, provide them with one of the following
first lines and work together to create a group poem. It is a great col-
laborative effort that allows them not only to work together, but also
to hear one another's ideas and voices.

I am leaving...
And I will tell you who I am...
I am hiding...
I have seen...
I have heard...
I have tasted...
I sing of...
I love the way...
I am lonesome for...
I remember...

Wait for...
See the...
Listen to...
Smell the...
Taste the...
Follow the...
Open the door to...
Sing a song of...
Night is the place where...

Starting with *These I have loved*, one class wrote the following poem:

These I have loved
The soft looseness of an old cotton sweatshirt
Wet footprints after the first snow
The newborn grass of spring
My birthday cake and Grandma's cookies
A country lane after a spring rain
Listening to a brook gurgling in the night
Faded jeans and love notes
Cool water that soothes a sore throat

I love the softness of an old pillow
Running in the crisp, clean morning air
The smell of freshly baked bread
Listening to people talk
The touch of baby kittens
Getting a tan
Brand new uniforms and Nike shoes
The scares on Halloween
And dusk on cold January nights

I love the thrill of the hunt
Quick glances looking for the prize
Swimming pools, shorts and bikes
Fresh cooked food on winter holidays
Crystals of white snow blowing
Visitors and H.B.O.
The smell of freshly cut grass
Cowboys and home

Or how about extra-spicy, extra-cheesy pizza
Money that never comes to an end
The northern lights on the Fourth of July
The smell of freshly picked strawberries
The sun smiling down on my fishing rod

All these I have loved.

—Group poem from *Prairie Winds*, Rapid City, South Dakota

5. HELPING BEGINNERS

How do we help very young children—kindergartners, first graders and second graders—write poems, especially the kind that do not rhyme? One way is to talk about a motivating topic, then write a group poem on the board as they contribute and discuss ideas.

A group of students in grades kindergarten through grade two wrote the following group poem with me as we discussed the imminent arrival of spring. We simply and with great joy spoke about all the wonderful things of which we become aware in that new, joyous season. I gave them the first line and called on the students to think of what they see, hear, feel, taste and smell when spring arrives.

Welcome, spring!
Open the windows!
Come in, spring smells—sweet flowers and rain.
Come in, furry deer, woolly sheep, shouting children.
Come in, bright daffodils, tulips and daisies.
Come in, little bugs and beautiful butterflies!
Come in, sunshine and warm spring rains.
Open the windows—
Spring is here!

As we wrote, gathering energy with each new line, we read aloud, first just the original line, then the first two lines, then three and so on. When we finished, we read the entire poem with great gusto, the children nearly shouting at the end, "Spring is here!" It was *their* poem. The teacher who writes such a poem with students must be enthusiastic and eager to create poetry with them, must "let go" and plunge into the fun of creating.

Question-and-answer poems

Students might establish a pattern in one poem and use it in several others. For example, discuss what it might be like to be a tree. Ask your students to stand, to bend, to stretch and to imagine being trees. Then write. In the following poem, the tree answers the poets' questions.

Oh tree, oh tree,
How does it feel always to stand in one place?
Oh tree, oh tree,
How does it feel to have squirrels run up your trunk?
Oh tree, oh tree,
How do you like having birds sing from your branches?

Oh girl, oh girl,
I wish I could run!
Oh girl, oh girl,
Squirrels' toes tickle my bark,
And the singing makes me happy all over.

Students can create their own questions and answers, adding those to the tree poem. Have them read their poem aloud over and over again as new lines are created.

Then you might give each child a small polished stone and invite them to write, alone or as a group, a poem to a stone, patterned after the tree poem.

Oh stone, oh stone,
Where have you been?
Oh stone, oh stone,
How does it feel to have people step on you?
Oh stone, oh stone, what do you see under the ground?
I will carry you in my pocket.

Oh boy, oh boy,
I have been everywhere.
Oh boy, oh boy,
I don't mind people stepping on me,
For I am hard and strong.
Oh boy, oh boy,
I saw lovely colored stones in the dirt underground,
And I will love being safe with you.

These small writers might write a poem to a carrot, to the rain, to a teddy bear, to a bicycle, to a worn favorite blanket, to a mother, a dad, an aunt or an uncle. One boy wrote a poem to green vegetables. (He didn't like them!)

Similes and metaphors for beginners

Young children literally think and talk in similes and metaphors, creating relationships and associations as easily as they talk and play. For children, language is a toy with which to play; it also is an instrument for exploring, for communicating. Indeed, language is an important way for them to discover who they are and to tell us who they are, to speak of what they want and know and dream. We all have heard children pretending:

I'm a lion! Hear me growl!
I'm a bird. Watch me fly!
I'm a big truck! See me go fast!

Children often speak in metaphors. They can extend metaphors to pattern poems after this example:

The first line begins with metaphor:
Today I am a lion

Ask students, "What are you doing, Ms. Lion?" Children will add movement to the poem:
Creeping through the jungle.

Ask, "What sound do you make?" Children will add sound:
Growwwwwll! Growwwwwll!
Hear me roar!

Now read the poem aloud together as one piece:

Today I am a lion
creeping through the jungle.
Growwwwwll! Growwwwwll!
Hear me roar!

Try another:
I'm a lovely yellow bird

Ask, "What are you doing, Mr. Bird?"
Flying through the trees.

Again, students add movement and sound:
Awwwkk! Awwkk!
How beautifully I sing!

Then again, read the poem aloud together as one piece:

I'm a lovely yellow bird
Flying through the trees.
Awwwkk! Awwkk!
How beautifully I sing!

Students may "be" inanimate objects: a swing or a door, for example. Add movement and sound to create a simple poem.

The softest things I know

Make a list of some of the softest things children can name: babies'
cheeks, kittens' noses, fluffy feathers, new green grass and so on.
Then put them into a poem.

> *The softest things I know are*
> *new babies' cheeks*
> *kittens' tiny noses*
> *fluffy yellow feathers on wee baby chicks*
> *new green blades of grass in spring*
> *gently blowing breezes*
> *smiles on the faces of my friends and*
> *cuddling in my grandma's lap*
> *The softest things I know*

Make other lists from which to draw poems: the happiest things I
know, the biggest things, the wiggliest things, the loudest things, the
stickiest things, and so on.

Using their third eye

Poetry requires imagination. Invite students to close their eyes as
you read to them poems that paint pictures in their "third eye," the eye
of imagination. Ask them to raise their hands when they can "see" in
their imaginations the picture painted by the poem. Then invite students to write their own poems, painting pictures with describing
words. Suggest that they close their eyes and *imagine* as you read this
poem:

> *At night*
> *snowflakes fall*
> *silently*
> *and all our town is*
>   *sleeping.*

> *There's nothing outside but the*
> *moon's reflection*
> *on our glittering glass*
> *pond*
> *and*
> *mouse-sized f o   p r i*
>   *o t   n t s   a   i*
>   *d   n c   n g*

>   *through the snow.*

Show students how the poet lets her audience *feel the feeling* of the
quiet night by making one thing—the mouse's footprints—stand out.
As students listen to one another's poems, ask what lines, phrases or
words catch their attention. Together, take note of these and discuss
reasons why they are effective. For example, how or why does the word
dancing stay in your mind after reading this poem?

Say it again!

Ask students to write down something their parents say over and over: "Brush your teeth," for example. "Pick up your toys." "Wear your mittens." "Take off your shoes." Each of these phrases can be a "jumper cable" to a poem.

Other beginnings: "Tell me about..."
                 "I want to hear..."

Quiet

"Quiet"
says the teacher teaching a lesson
"Quiet"
says the librarian checking in books
"Quiet"
says my sister talking on the phone
"Quiet"
says my brother watching TV
"Quiet"
I say, is far from me!

—Allison Bittner, grade 5

Pocket poems

Carry copies of some of your favorite poems in your pockets. Trade them with students for copies of their own favorites—poems they have written themselves are wonderfully acceptable. Ask students to read these poems aloud to you before you put them in your own pocket!

6. POETS WORKING TOGETHER

Since poetry is meant to be read aloud as well as silently, we must create opportunities for that to happen. Provide tape recorders so students can read their favorite poems aloud, listen to themselves, become their own "first audience." It may be that what they read aloud is not exactly what they thought they had written, and reading aloud may lead students to revise their poems to make them clearer.

Students can help one another with their reading aloud by listening to others' poems, suggesting where the poets might emphasize words or phrases by reading them softly or loudly, or by pausing for emphasis before or after a word. It might be helpful for students to have copies of others' poems and mark on those copies helpful suggestions for reading them aloud—places where reading should be louder or softer, and so on.

As you and your students write and read poetry, be sure to model by writing your own poetry on the board. Allow your students to see you develop ideas, work with them, and finally write down your final poems as you want them to be.

"Shaping" poems can be fun

On the board, show students how to write poems in shapes. By playing with their poems, adding detail and drawings, students can present them attractively on paper. Most often, it is easier for students to write the poem first, then arrange it into the desired shape. Computers offer a way to produce clean, sharp copies of poems, but a poem printed in the poet's own hand, perhaps enhanced with line drawings, is sometimes preferable to printed pages that all look rather alike.

Snow

SNOW
The snow Falls I want to go out
and Play in the cold snow.
Sometimes I can Feel the
cold snow on my Face
It tingles a bit. Let It
SNOW!

—Jamie, grade 5

Questions can help students get started

Suggest that your students think about a peaceful, quiet place. Ask, "Where is it? Is it night or day? What time is it? Who is there? What is happening? What feelings are in that place?" Tell them to include two comparisons in their poems using similes or metaphors. When the poems are finished, students should cover their ears and read to themselves aloud, softly, what they have written. Are there unnecessary words that can be left out? Are there generic words that can be replaced by specific, clear, extraordinary words? Suggest that students use onomatopoeia to create sound in the poem.

Now you might suggest that students write a poem about a noisy place. How would the questions from the quiet poem above change for a noisy poem? Again, suggest using onomatopoeia to create sound in the poem.

Write it all down

Suggest that your students keep notebooks in which they write words, phrases and poetry ideas that can be used for writing poems to be written at another time. Remind them that wonderful ideas fly out of our heads as quickly as they enter and that writing them down will ensure they are not lost.

Making poems *shine*

Be sure students read each completed poem aloud to themselves. Remind them to *think* as they listen; to use words that *show* rather than tell; to use *extraordinary* adjectives; to use only carefully chosen adverbs, to use strong nouns. It is hard to find images in one's mind for *stuff*, for example, but *red and black checkered skating socks* paints a clear picture. Show students how to leave out unimportant words like *a*, *an*, and *the*; and how to change generic words like *went* to sharp, lively words like *raced, rocketed, turtled, crept, flew*; and how to arrange words on the page to *look like a poem*.

Students should read their poems again and again to see if they say exactly what they want them to say.

In other words

Brainstorm with students other words for nouns—for instance, other words for *fog*—curtain, blanket, sheet, wall. Adding well-chosen adjectives—*grey swirling curtains of fog*, for example—creates new images of fog that may work in their poems. Class exercises like this, in which students and teacher brainstorm together, can help even the most reluctant writer feel ready to begin. Be sure thesauruses are available, preferably one in every student's desk.

Celebrating—Hooray for poems and those who write them!

•When poems are finished, it's time to celebrate. You might present an evening of readings, inviting parents and friends to come and listen. It might also be fun to do a morning or afternoon poetry reading for another class.

•Friday-afternoon poetry readings can provide a great ending to the school week. Students can draw numbers or volunteer to read their poems to the class during perhaps the last fifteen minutes of the day.

•You might present students with their own individual audio tapes, inviting them to record on the tapes each finished poem. These go home with students at the end of the year.

•If your students are present at parent conferences, provide them with the opportunity to read aloud one or two of their own poems to their parents. It reinforces their confidence as writers and allows parents to see them at their very best as performers of their own writing.

•Your class might want to create a class book of poems. A design committee might plan a special cover, and each student, perhaps with feedback from classmates, might choose several poems for inclusion in the book.

•Your class might choose to create, instead of a book, a "big box of poetry." Fill the box with the students' poems, each printed neatly on a large card. Then provide a few minutes every day for students to draw favorites from the box and read them aloud to the class.

•Each student should have his or her own portfolio, folder or box of finished poems. Students will take great delight in seeing their collections grow, in realizing that they truly are poets who have written poems that are unique and important.

•Offer a variety of materials for students to use in illustrating, decorating, and designing their poems for publishing and displaying.

•Perhaps toward the end of the school year, allow each poet his or her own day as *poet in residence*. You might provide a special "poet's chair" (rocking chairs are favorites!) from which to read. "I still remember my day as poet in residence," says a now college graduate. "I felt so special, reading my own poems to my classmates, and they were a very appreciative audience because they had written poems of their own, just as I had."

Tell your students: In your poems, write about what you know, about what you think, about what you feel, about what you wonder. Be yourself. You don't have to imitate other poets. Your poems are as wonderful as theirs. Find new ways to say what you have inside you, ways no one has discovered before.

Encourage your students to *play* with poetry. Tell them, "Have fun with poetry; the poems you write belong to *you*."

Above all, give them permission to write freely in an atmosphere that is encouraging, accepting, and understanding of each child and his or her abilities, interests and concerns. We never can know how the language of poetry will serve our students as they move through our classrooms and on into lives away from us. It may be that the time spent talking, reading, and writing poetry together is, for many students, the most important time of all.

7. TEACHERS, LET'S TALK!

I had been leading a discussion about poetry with a class of students and their teacher, and they had been writing their own poems and were sharing them. After several students had shared theirs, the teacher raised his hand. "I'd like to share mine," he said quietly.

"Covers on my bed," he began.
"Covers on my bed
snuggly
toasty warm on a cold winter night.
Covers on my bed
protection from
the big bad bogeyman."

Tears began creeping down his cheeks.

"Covers on my bed
love
as Dad and Mom tuck me in.
Covers on my bed
bright and blue
highways that I run my toys on.

Covers on my bed
the tent
my friend and I play in.
Covers on my bed
what Mom tells me to make
every morning."

—L. Peder Larson, Teacher

His students listened, many of them with tears in their eyes too, as they realized that precious memories prompted his gentle poem.

Why does poetry have power to make us cry? I think it is because in poetry, we speak important truths. We say what *is*; we don't talk around it. We don't write *about* a feeling—we write *the feeling* onto paper. The act of creating poetry is meaningful for the poet. It comes from deep inside us, and when a poet writes from the heart, others hear and understand. We do not write poems to meet someone else's expectations or to fit another's predetermined goal for what will be written, but to speak of our *selves*.

The woman was a member of a teachers' summer workshop. We had talked about writing poetry and she was hesitant about much of what we discussed. She wasn't sure she agreed with my giving the class permission to leave out capitals and punctuation if they chose. I wanted them to feel free to play with their poems, to enjoy writing as they took their blankets (their assignment for the day was to provide their own blanket) out onto the college campus and found inviting places under shady trees on that hot day. They had an hour and a half of quiet time for writing poems, then would come back and share something of their writing experiences.

I sat in the classroom writing my own poetry, available if anyone needed to talk. No one appeared for an hour and a half; then they began coming in. "How did it go?" I asked this lovely, reluctant writer. Her eyes shone as she spoke. "I surprised myself," she said softly.

Another teacher came in, exulting, "What a *gift*! A whole hour and a half for writing poetry! Wow! This was great!"

When everyone had returned, I asked who might like to share a poem from the afternoon's writing. "I will," said the writer who had been hesitant. She began reading:

The empty schoolyard
Lonely, empty space
forgotten bikes waiting for their owners
blue teeter-totters
banging up and down
blown by a ghostly wind
silent echoes of children shouting
left over from the weeks before
swings with their empty canvas seats
blowing in the breeze

Will I be this empty when I must leave?

—Eleanor Klostergaard, Teacher

As she came to the end of her poem, tears began streaming down her face. We had thought she was writing about the summer vacation just begun, but her poem was much deeper than that, we knew, as she read the last line: *Will I be this empty when I must leave?* And she confided in us her love of teaching, her dread of the day she must retire.

Often, as teachers begin discovering their poets' voices, tears fall while they write. In one group, several of them began wiping their eyes as they wrote. One hurried off to the restroom to wash her face, then came back, beaming. "I'm writing a wonderful poem!" she said, for all to hear.

When it was time to share, each was eager to read aloud one or two new creations. We all understood when each of the first three readers wept as she read, stopped to catch her breath, saying, "Just a minute." "I can *do* this!" "Please wait—I want to read this myself," and proceeded to finish the reading. They took great pleasure in hearing themselves read aloud what their poets' hearts had written. The fourth teacher got up to read, burst into tears and then laughed until she cried some more. "I don't know why *I'm* crying!" she said. "*My* poem isn't even sad!" Then we all laughed again. There is something about the language of poetry that is hard to put into words—but we all saw and heard it as they shared their wonderful poems.

At another teachers' session, we had finished our discussion of poetry, talking about the freedom of writing without rhyme and syllabic requirements. I had read to our group of teachers a number of poems as they jotted down thoughts that could be turned into poems of their own. Now it was time to write. The room grew quiet; the only sound to be heard was that of pens and pencils moving across papers. After perhaps fifteen minutes of writing, I asked, "How are you coming?'

While most nodded their heads and commented, "Just fine," one teacher raised his hand. "I can't get started," he said. "I can't move beyond my list to write a poem."

Another teacher responded with a kind smiie. "I think you're scared," said this second male teacher. "It's hard when there's not the structure we're used to." He encouraged the other teacher to keep trying. Others in the room nodded in agreement.

When all our lives we've been taught to write only the structured, rhyming poetry, this new poetry can be intimidating. I think it is easier for students to write this kind of poetry than it is for us, because they do not carry with them a lifetime of only the other kind.

Don't give up! Be gentle with yourself, and try your poetry voice in small ways—a simple line or two that pleases you can be your beginning. The second teacher, who had helped the first, left that initial poetry session with this sweet poem about his grandfather:

For my grandpa
The Old Thresher
enveloped his
silo in the woods
with
space dancing.

—Craig A. Nelson, Teacher

Models!

Did you ever have a teacher who wrote and shared stories, poems, essays, reports with your class? Did you ever have a teacher who was moved to tears by reading his or her own poetry to you? Few of us did, and if we did, we remember that teacher, that most special occurrence. Now we know we must model those things that we want children to learn. This means we too must write. Let your students see you writing poetry. Just as they read aloud what they have written, share what you write too. Let children respond to your poems as they do to those of their classmates. They will love hearing your poet's voice.

The atmosphere changes in classrooms where teachers share learning experiences with students. The teacher who instructs students to write poems but never writes one has no idea of the effort put into the writing; no sense of the relief of pouring onto paper the loneliness or happiness, the sadness or deep gratefulness we all feel in our lives; no understanding of the triumph of accomplishment experienced by a writer who has successfully put his or her thoughts on paper in a poem. There is a "high" that goes with reading aloud one's poetry to other poets that is like no other—teachers must experience that too.

Sometimes, as in the poems for my grandma and for my dad, lines of poetry come nearly finished almost before I can write them down. That is the poem demanding to be written. It is much different than, for example, an assignment given by a teacher to "write a poem about rain." One of my students told me about a poetry session in her sixth-grade class. "Today we will write poems about the sun," said the teacher. "As we talked," said my friend, "I had a poem growing inside me about a *bird*, not about the sun. I told my teacher I really wanted to write a poem about a bird. So then she asked how many other kids wanted to write about a bird instead of the sun. About half of them chose *bird*, so she said, 'Well then, today we'll all write poems about the sun, and tomorrow we'll all write poems about birds.'"

"She didn't get it," said the girl. "I needed to write about a bird *then*, not when *she* decided it was time!"

The teacher who knows the Muse, the teacher who *must* write poetry, understands that one does not *assign* students the writing of a poem about a given topic, but instead *invites* students to write what is inside them.

Finding their voices, singing their songs

I was writer-in-residence at an elementary school where a sixth-grade boy wrote a wonderful poem about deer hunting. In the poem, the eyes of the young hunter (the boy) meet the eyes of the deer and the hunter wonders about the deer's family, just as he thinks of his own. In the end, the hunter directs his bullets straight down into the ground and goes home happy that he did not kill the deer.

I complimented the young poet on his fine poem and asked him to make a copy for me during the day. Later I visited with the computer instructor who told me she was putting together a school newspaper, having students copy into the paper their favorite poems from library books. I suggested using instead poems written that day by the school's own sixth-grade poets and told her about the wonderful hunting poem. "Oh!" she exclaimed. "That must have been the boy who came tearing into the computer room this noon. He said he had written a great poem. Whenever he's in computer class, he complains that typing on the keyboard is too hard for him, that we go way too fast. Today he said it was *easy* to find the right keys. He sat down and typed that poem into the computer and ran it off so fast I couldn't believe it! You know," she added, "he's new to our school and hasn't made new friends here yet. The move has been difficult for him and everything in school seems so hard." But his poem *sang!* Again and again it happens: Many students find their voices, sing their songs, in poetry.

We *play* with poetry. We help students begin, perhaps give them some ideas with which to start. Then we let them write. Often it is these children, each gifted with his or her own unique voice, who say in poetry things that make us weep and laugh, that let us get to know them.

Those of us who live in towns and cities often believe that children who live on farms are inured to those things that might be difficult for us to see, that births and deaths of animals are viewed as commonplace—something farm families accept without emotion. And yet, following the reading of some poems about farms, three farm boys from three different small towns wrote poems about farming:

Bad farmer
Kill the cow and starve the horse!
Crack the eggs and set chickens on fire!
Melt the tractor and burn the crops!
Knock down the sheds and the barn!
Blow up the elevators and bins!
Cover the land with toxic waste!
Start the tree rows on fire!
Do you think I shouldn't be a farmer?

—Andrew Gjovik, grade 5

Farming
Cows and pigs
die
while I watch
helplessly
as mean men
shoot them down
in the graying
land
and drop them
from the sky
from the barn
covered with
red

—Jesse Carsten, grade 6

Farming
Cows in the barn are silent.

You hear tractors roaring up
and down the field,
Kids in the pig barn trying to
catch a squealing, screaming
pig,

The smell of new baked rolls
for the farmers,

Dirt crunching under wheels,

Old barns sitting there
unused, sagging by the unused
field,

Fragrant, new-cut hay in the fields

But the farmers take their guns to
the barn and that's when I cover my
ears and eyes
and go crying to my
mom. I'm trying to think of
something else.
Tomorrow I won't find all of them
there. I'll go back to take the garbage to
the burning pit and see all the cows
lying there
dead.

—Jeremy Bursell, grade 6

In what other way could these young poets have spoken with such eloquence? They found the words in poetry.

Renowned poet Rainer Maria Rilke, writing in 1903 to young aspiring poet Franz Kappus, said: "...try, like some first human being, to say what you see and experience and love and lose...seek those (themes) which your own everyday life offers you; describe your sorrows and desires, passing thoughts and the belief in some sort of beauty—describe all these with loving, quiet, humble sincerity, and use, to express yourself, the things in your environment, the images from your dreams, and the objects of your memory." The three boys whose poems speak so clearly of what they know have done exactly as Rilke advised, and their poems are stunning.

Writing with a class of sixth graders, I watched a girl creating a poem about dreams of lovely things.

I dream, she wrote, of lazy, quiet lagoons,
I dream of beautiful birds
I dream of tumbling waters

     and more...

Across the room, a boy also was writing a poem about dreams. I found it extremely interesting, as no mention had been made of dreams during the entire class discussion. When the writing stopped, both students were eager to share their dream poems. They were exquisite, and we told them so.

When the class ended, the teacher followed me out of the room and down the hall, with puzzlement and excitement written all over her face. "You have no idea what just happened here!" she said. "Those two students have been terribly abused. Where did those poems come from?" Where, indeed? For some reason known only to them, and independently of one another, they chose to write something beautiful. I prayed as I left that school that those two students would know where to find words to soothe their pain.

I was speaking at a young authors' conference, teaching a class on the writing of poetry to sixth- and seventh-grade students. Each was there because he or she had selected this particular class—they were there by choice.

In the middle of the room was a small, fragile-looking boy. His blonde hair was disheveled, his face pale and thin, his clothing faded and old. He watched me from the corners of tired, sad eyes as I talked about poetry. He stared at the ceiling, curled himself down into his seat and gazed out the window. He seemed to be listening intently, but while the others took copious notes, he wrote nothing. I wondered what he would do when it was time to begin writing, as the poems were to originate from the list of notes students jotted down as I read to them. Interesting—this had not happened before in one of my poetry workshops, a student's total inactivity while we were getting ready to write.

I finished speaking and the students looked through their brainstorming, each chose an idea for a poem and began to write. As I roamed the room, I could see that he too was writing. I glanced around to see what students were putting on their papers. I came toward his seat from the back; he was unaware of my presence. His hand was moving quickly across the paper. I looked down and saw the title: "The dark, dark room."

in the dark, dark room
there is no happiness,
only sadness
only loneliness.
in the dark, dark room
only sadness is there behind the door

On he wrote, pouring his sadness onto paper. While others were eager to share their finished poems, he folded his tightly and held it against his chest. I wanted to tell him how wonderful his poem was, but clearly, right then, no one was allowed to approach that small, pained *self*. But he had written, perhaps for the first time, what he felt inside.

The class period ended and he was gone, a small, most unlikely poet. I hoped that he would go home and write onto paper more of himself; clearly, he possessed the *voice of a poet*.

In another school, writing with fourth graders and fifth graders, something wonderful happened. I had read, and the students had jotted ideas from which they would create poems. They began writing, and as I walked around, peeking over shoulders to see how they were doing, I observed one boy writing an incredibly beautiful poem about the waters of two streams racing, pounding down the mountains and hillsides to form one exquisitely clear, sparkling river. It was striking in its effect, the work of a true poet.

During our writing, two teachers sat in the back of the room, and despite the fact that I had invited them to write too, they were busy recording grades in little red books and whispering loudly to one another.

When several students had completed their poems, I invited those who wished to share to raise their hands. Among those volunteering to read was the creator of the poem about the streams and the river. Now the two teachers were listening, and when I called on that poet to read his poem, they smirked at one another, as though to say, "*Him? Can he do anything right?*" The looks on their faces made me angry. Then the poet began to read, and their jaws dropped.

I could have cheered out loud. *Look!* I wanted to say. *This child is filled with poetry!*

Poetry is not only what happens on paper, but what happens within us as we write it and read it. Poetry makes more clear the worlds inside us and around us, and it helps us understand the worlds in which others live as well. Something happened in that classroom. As the poet read, not only his classmates, but his teachers, looked at him in awe. He was *somebody*, and he knew it.

This is why we *must* let our students learn how to write poetry, because it may be the best way—it may be the only way—they can convey their worlds, can tell us who they are.

Nurturing yourself as writer

My love of poetry has been nurtured in many ways, by many people. One of them, a professor at the college my daughter attended, is renowned for her poetry readings. Each time I attended a mother-daughter weekend there, this lover of language read some of her favorite poetry to us. Her readings prompted me to invite all my guests to a spring luncheon to bring a favorite poem to share. Listening to her read also sent me once again to bookstore shelves to search for some of her favorite poets and propelled me into used bookstores to search out some of those older, hard-to-find ones.

If of thy mortal goods thou art bereft,
And from thy slender store two loaves alone
to thee are left,
Sell one, and with the dole
Buy hyacinths to feed thy soul.

—Gulistan of Moslith Eddin Saadi

And oh, I would buy books of poetry!

A well-known Midwestern writer says that a poet is being a poet only in the act of writing a poem. I think the poet also is *being a poet* when someone else reads and responds to the poem he or she has created, when two minds touch through the writing of one. Few poets acquire monetary wealth through the writing of poetry, but oh, some things are more valuable than money!

The process presented in this book, starting with discussion of what poetry is and can be, then listening to and demonstrating model poems as students begin to write, can help you, as teacher and poet, introduce the writing of poetry to your students, can help you continue to encourage and draw them into this significant way of writing themselves onto paper.

Poetry is more than mimicking someone else's example. It is using your own ideas, going off on your own into the great expanse of creative freedom of which each of us capable.

Some suggestions for writing poetry
• Write about what you know and feel deeply.
• Show, don't tell; let words paint the pictures.
• Be specific, be clear—don't be generic!
• Leave room for your audience to imagine, to feel something left unsaid.
• Use strong nouns—don't be wishy-washy!
• Use extraordinary adjectives.
• Use lively verbs and few adverbs.
• Let each poem rest a day or more, then read it again. Polish it until it shines.
• Read your poem aloud. How does it sound?
• On paper, give it the look of a poem.
• Read it aloud to yourself, then to friends and family. Read it over and over again. Listen to the sound of your wonderful poem, and name yourself again: *poet*.
• When a line comes into your head, write it down. It may be a last line, a middle line, a first line. No matter. Save it. Put it in your poetry notebook and it will be waiting there when you need it.
• Use new, fresh words of your own; don't fall back on clichés.

One of a kind
In these days of computerized printouts, it is easy to make perfect final copies of poems in snappy black print on snowy white paper. Sometimes it is more interesting to see poems written in students' (or your own!) best handwriting, perhaps accented with simple doodles or drawings in colored pencil or pen. That also reflects the poet. Do your own doodling too.

Poetry in motion
When I was a child we spent many hours lying on the soft grass of my cousin's farm in the country. We gazed up at the white, puffy clouds by day and looked for shapes in them—big, fat pillows, soaring birds, wonderful dark thunderclouds. We felt the soft green grass beneath us like new blankets spread all over the yard for our own personal use. By night we counted the stars, searched for the constellations we'd heard of but always had trouble finding. Those were poetry moments, poetry hours, because the pure feeling of those times lived inside us. We internalized what was happening, understood completely the experience of the moment. Sometimes we danced in the moonlight, ran and skipped in the rain. Our joy, our dancing and skipping, was poetry too.

We recently watched on television a woman whose husband had just successfully undergone the terrifying, exciting experience of having heart transplant surgery. Informed by the doctors that he had come through the operation successfully and was doing well, this ecstatic woman went skipping down the hospital corridors, joyously greeting everyone she met: "Thank you! Thank you! Thank you!" To the orderlies, the nurses, to visitors. "Thank you!" Then she spun around mid-skip to exult, "Thank you, *World* !" That was poetry.

Poetry is personal, sometimes nearly ineffable. It is *ours*. Some time ago I submitted a poem to the editor of a poetry publication. He wrote back that he would publish my poem if only I would leave out the last line. *The last line? What? That was the most important line of all! And it was* mine! I tore up his letter, posted my poem on my own bulletin board and mentally informed the editor that I was not about to change it for any amount of money. He had no idea what that poem, what that last line meant to me. We must remember that students' poems are that precious to them as well, and we must remember to speak gently, understandingly with them about their poems as together we consider changes that might make their poems stronger.

How does a poem begin? I think that when we have invited poetry into our lives, when we are reading and writing poems, something happens: We see or feel or hear something that speaks to us—a memory, a clear thought—and suddenly we have a new insight, knowledge of what we want our poem to say. When we are attuned to poetry, it arrives.

The Park Hotel
They sold my life today
The auctioneer raised his gavel and pounded the blow
A hundred years of history lost except for my memories
No more the wide cement porch
where old people rocked and we roller-skated
No more the aging lobby where my brother and I
competed shooting his BB gun
The empty third floor where we were scared
by a ghost
No more put-together rooms of our apartment
I'll never get to curl up and read
in the window seat again
Never look out my bedroom window
to reassure our dogs
Who will climb my willow tree
to strip for Indian gum?
run to catch a ride on a baggage car?
Gone is our ancient bellhops' comforting presence
My mother's lament—But we don't have a house—
was not echoed by us.
Our hotel was our Beloved Home!

—Cindy Karner, Teacher

Cindy's poem came to her as she jotted down memories from her childhood. When she read it to those of us in her class, she wept, and we wept with her: It was her own life of which she wrote, her deepest feelings poured into poetry.

Don't overanalyze

We must be careful not to kill students' pleasure in poetry by always insisting that they "Find four metaphors in this poem" or "Look for an example of personification" in it. Instead, we must offer them regularly a smorgasbord of poems of all kinds from which they may choose those they love, those that speak especially to them, those that may stimulate them to write poems of their own.

Find this book

If you buy no other book about poetry for your own enjoyment, one that you can share with your students, I recommend Paul B. Janeczko's *The Place My Words Are Looking For* (Simon & Schuster). It contains wonderful poems by and information about thirty-nine of our country's leading poets. Every poet in the book has something special to say to us about poetry. Each poem in the collection is appealing and unique. I purchased my own copy on the recommendation of a fifth grader who came tearing into our classroom one day, nearly bursting with enthusiasm: "Oh, Mrs. B! You've got to buy this new book! You'll love it!" I did buy it, I do love it and I recommend it.

My poetry box

"I have something for you!" my friend said excitedly as we finished our telephone conversation. "I'll give it to you tomorrow!"

At dinner the next evening, she presented me with something wonderful: a custom-made poetry box created just for me! It was an oval box, about eight inches long and four inches high. It had been painted dark green and covered with pictures of frogs, my favorite creatures, and flowers and lily pads, then covered with several clear coats of a protective material. Inside were small wooden blocks with words in decoupage on them—*purple*, *painting*, *footprints*, *grain*—and more, and seashells and small wooden hearts, also with words attached—words to get me thinking. The inside of the box too was covered with pictures—teapots, yarn (I enjoy knitting), books and dolls, all special interests of mine. I had never seen anything like it before.

"It's a poetry box," said my friend. "to help you get started writing poems."

It was intriguing—and I tried it the next day. Just as we go from concrete to abstract in our learning, so the concrete—blocks, seashells and words—stimulated me to go into my own faraway place and write my first poem "from the poetry box"—a song to a frog.

Heidi Howell, creator of poetry boxes, says, "I was first introduced to the idea of a poet's box by Carolyn Forche, who uses a similar technique in her experimental poetry workshops. Her box, however, is often designed to be a reflection of the poet: the outside of the box represents the poet's conscious or surface material concerns; the inside represents the poet's heart/soul/unconscious. I needed a generative tool, so I adapted her design to fit my needs by including material (both inside and outside the boxes—without distinction) which I found interesting and inspirational. The box then becomes more than a reflection of me (although this element surely remains), but also a poke or prod to get me to write—to surprise and delight me into poetry." Howell's love of poetry is catching—her mother has been drawn into making poetry boxes too, and it was she who created mine.

Your students might create poetry boxes, putting inside them things that represent their own unique interests. These might be traded with classmates, allowing others to respond to the unique things in each box.

Summing up

In writing poetry like this with thousands of students, I have learned something that is consistently true: It is often the child who has the hardest time learning, the child who is most misunderstood, the child who seems unable to do anything well, the child who is saddest, the child who is angriest, the child who is loneliest, and the child who hurts who finds her or his strong voice in writing wonderful, important poetry that *rocks* us as we listen.

We take away the rules for writing essays and reports. We say, "In this kind of writing you don't need to worry about punctuation or complete sentences. You don't even have to use capital letters if you don't want to. You are free to write what you feel, what you know, what you see, what you think, what you hear, what you dream, what you are." We give them permission to write themselves onto paper. Doing this with a class of students who had been described to me as "learning disabled," I heard an audible sigh of relief as I informed the students that they did not have to start each line with a capital letter, use punctuation marks or complete sentences. They turned and grinned at their teacher when I said they had permission to start their poems with the words *and* or *but*. Then they proceeded with gusto to write poems of themselves, poems that made the adults in their room feel what they were feeling.

This can happen for you too, for yourself and for your students. Use the teachers' poems that follow to jumpstart yourself into writing your own poems. Then share poems from the student anthology with your students as they begin to write theirs.

I wish you joys, surprises and great fulfillment as you step into the rich, colorful world of poetry.

8. POETRY SAMPLER— TEACHERS' POEMS

(all-)Night talk
school-talk, men-talk,
God-talk passed between us—
five flannel-gowned, quilted-warm,
almost-women—drifting
on a borrowed waterbed.
Never more gentle,
never more sure,
our futures hugged us in the dark.
The night rode easy,
toward Saturday morning,
our tomorrows, our next years.
We thought each other beautiful
and slept a sound morning as
the sun came pink,
over rooftops
through windows
on our faces.

—Gabi Kirsch

Anonymity at the 10 o'clock show
No one knows me here.
That tastes as good to me as
the salty kernels I crunch
between my teeth.
I'm beautiful, invisible,
glad just being in the dark
living vicariously through the Them on the screen.
We cry together, yell,
laugh.
They spill their guts to me and
I'm grateful.
I remain until the very last, watching
the credits run.
Stumbling post-movie steps, like
half-a-drunken stupor, up the aisle,
I am watched for my reaction
by the next-in-lines.
But I reveal nothing; I won't share.
Let them choose for themselves.
For just now, I chose a movie,
solitude, anonymity.

—Gabi Kirsch

Auction
Treasures
 Whose were they?
 Worth much to someone
 Worth nothing to dealers
Junk
 Dirty, musty, moldy
 Broken and ugly
 I won't bid!
 $2,000—and it still has holes

SOLD!

—Nancy Newman

Cemetery seasons

Spring
green hope
bluebird of happiness
daffodil and crocus
among the dead
young hope
young life
forever vanished
joy and laughter
buried
silence
summer
slumbers
robin Redbreast
roses and daisies
what's in a name
families
long remembered
the world turns
silence
autumn
haze of smoke
departing geese
urgent cries
unheard
dust to dust
returns
silence
winter bleak...blank
cardinal poinsettia
blood heart
against the snow
comforts of the deep
eternity
unchanging
silence

—Marilyn Nelson

Christmas
Hustle bustle
Hurry scurry
too rushed to enjoy
Red and green traffic lights
flashing in soft falling snow.
Department store Santas clanging
golden brass bells
last-minute shoppers rushing
to seize the perfect gift
Finally the cookies are baked
the turkey is stuffed and
I can lie peacefully by
the warm blazing fire
gaze at the feathered angel
on top of the tree
Savor the long-awaited calm
and quietly celebrate Him—
the true meaning of Christmas.

—Nancy Stevens

Coffee cups
and we came too late
you had gone, they said
dead
just minutes before
they had taken you away
in a screaming black car
rushing toward
confirmation
that you were dead
really dead
but I went
upstairs and
there by your chair
sat your coffee cup
and I picked it up and
it was just barely warm and I
took a sip

and maybe that is why when I
drink coffee I
always wrap my hands
around the cup
to feel the heat
and see if my cup
is still warm

too   —Joyce Bumgardner

Cosmos

newcomer in the perennial bed
outsize
grabbing precious space
pushing
shoving
smaller plants bullied by your
demands for attention
they'll be back next
year
       you won't!

—Vivian Nelson

Directions
    North to my parents'
South to my in-laws'
    East to my friend's
West to my sister's

Floating around under a dome
    being stretched
The compass of my life.

—Beth Huntley

The first day
I arise.

No longer can I seek shelter
in
darkness

I move slowly
not with purpose
but with hesitation

The light increases
uncovers my plans
sparse, naked

I hear the rumble of distant voices
growing louder, relentless

I yield to its demands
open the door
The fragile silence of the morning is
broken

Faces rush at me
defiant, bold, honest
challenging me to teach
when I
have so much to
learn.

—Roland Huyen

Following Susannah
We are the tourists
who have stepped off our ship
to see your country.

"Stay in a straight line," you instruct firmly,
your crisp Mexican accent,
your fine young beauty delighting us.
We, your seniors, giggle and
snap our ragged line into a ruler-straight edge,
surprised to be first graders again.

We follow your bouncing black ponytail,
your shiny red tour guide's hat,
your red and white striped blouse
onto the rattly old bus.
Your teacher's voice points out those things
of which you are especially proud...
houses, cathedrals, schools, stores.
We look where you point, seeing the city
through your proud eyes.

"A straight line, please,"
you remind us, and we follow you
off the bus
through the courtyard
into the winery
up the stairs
along sampling tables
down the stairs
out the door,
back on the bus;
our straight line follows
wherever you lead.

"We are now at our beautiful city center,"
you announce, and we get off the bus,
moving in our nearly-straight line through the hallways,
exquisitely painted ceilings looking down on us.

Suddenly, you dismiss us.
We pause, puzzled children
given unexpected freedom.
"Enjoy your shopping.
Be back at the bus at 12:20."

For twenty-five minutes we scurry
up and down the streets
in and out of stores

gathering souvenirs,
first graders at recess,
snatching up pretty rocks.

It is 12:20.
We stand before the open bus door,
our line programmed ruler-straight.
The door closes and we rattle along
back to our ship.

"Thank you for coming with me to Me'hico,"
you say, smiling.

Off the bus,
our line wobbles apart
as we move toward our ship.

Looking back, we see your
ponytail dancing under your red hat
as you take your place before the
next group of tourists.
We giggle.
They do not know that soon they will be
first graders again,
following in a ruler-straight line
wherever you lead them.

—Joyce Bumgardner

Gift
A labyrinth of color fills the rug
each one appearing in a ritual of pattern
put there with a pair of gnarled, nurturing
hands
now cold.
The gift challenges the chill
with the warmth of a mother's selfless love
Love which is gone but
still here.

—Barbara Sigurdson

Grace sings

On this still, gloomy morning
no sound no sound no sound
even tree leaves shake silently in gray drizzly mist

suddenly

a burst of golden orange sweeps to the branch
outside my window
drinks the sweet nectar
then stops to trill its joyous yodel

an oriole blesses the morning.

Grace, I think, is this:
astonishing joy
a streak of golden orange
through dulling sameness

and on the next branch
waiting its turn
a hummingbird singing
for happy
with only the sound
of its
wings

—Joyce Bumgardner

Grandpa

I see your stone
telling the world
when you arrived
when you left
and I wonder
who you were
what were you like
as a baby
or little boy
as a man
Grandma's husband,
father and grandfather—
I wish I had known you
before you left.

Though when I think about it
I do know something
about who you were

from stories my father's told,
by the man my father has become,
from pictures in our family photo album.
I think you were caring,
lonely at times,
Raised by your sister
when your mother died
Concerned about family,
Giving what you could
to those in need,
raising two of your grandchildren
for awhile
Passing your love
to a new generation

I wonder what you
would have thought of me
You knew me so briefly before you
died.
I know you would have given me
your love
as you did the others
who came before me.
I wish, Grandpa,
you could have stayed
a little longer
in my world
so I could have
memories about you

to share with the others
To keep close to my heart
To help me feel your love
surrounding me
when I am sad
and feeling alone.

—Stephanie Hiatt

Growing up
She sits reading on the steps
immersed in a mystery.
My daughter's mind is
far away.

I see her long wavy hair catching
bright golden sunrays
reflecting

her soul.
The latest water bottle in her hand
symbol of being the older one
in a neighborhood of
noisy, playing children.

She impatiently waits for life to burst
while I sigh
with sadness.

I call her name—will she hear?
A distracted look...
...an annoyed response

I ache remembering the smile
beckoning strangers to her side
as we sailed down store aisles.

Her serious face turns toward me
and focuses on my sad one
and
her baby smile forms on her lips.
She jumps to give me a hug
dispels my fears.
She is here still
for a short while longer.

—Joyce Nilsen

Here come the clowns
Here come the clowns.
Smiling faces, frowning faces
Ever-changing emotions
Trusted with children of all ages
Here come the clowns.

Here come the clowns.
Hidden features, hidden emotions
Never revealing the truth
Trusted with children of all ages.
Here come the clowns.

—Ramona Quartier-Tschudy

Hope
That bed
That bitter pain-time
When days and moons
Came and
came

That bed
That chrysalis
Where pain spins its binding threads.
Like old skin
She sheds her dreams
And waits in lonely dark.

Still dawn
whispers to her.
Awkward she struggles...
Pushes through those sticky threads
Toward that hazed light
Escape!

Trust tender, fresh wings?
Fragile untested sings?
Escape!
Escape that bed
That empty shell.

From rose to daisy flits
In saffron gardens now
She flies
Resting on magenta velvet petals
Does not stay
But visits emerald places
Unseen
From that bed.

—Kathy Nelimark

I'll say I knew her then
Small hands like birds
flit back and forth,
then waver,
long enough for you to see
those tender fingertips
where the rest of the nails should be.
(She nibbles as she creates.)
"I don't want to be normal,"
she tells you seriously,
pulling a rabbit,
a jester,
a flamingo from her pen.
"I don't want the normal things
people are supposed to want."
Her hands fly again
shaping her dreams for you in the air
as if saying, "see, see."
She's grounded,
caged in her own creation.
Soon she'll paint the key:
hands flying,
ever so sweetly,
will carry her away.

—Gabi Kirsch

I want it!
kids happy with their lives
grandchildren always loved and safe
peace, not war
no more starvation, poverty or crime
homes for everyone
honest politicians
collaboration and cooperation at work
more time with relatives
a lean body
a better golf game
more creativity
a voice that sings like a bird
someone to do the cooking
houses that retire
vacations in winter
a house that stays clean
time alone at home
more leisure time
I want it!   —Dee Moriarty

Memories of an eclipse

Growing anticipation of a vanishing moon
 The spicy aroma of a leather jacket
Slowly being erased by earth
 A gentle arm around my waist
Night sounds magnified
 Perfect harmony
Brilliant, awe-inspiring crescent
 Speaking without words
Blackness
 Changed forever!

—Linda Lee Ahlers

Morning wake-up

Wakefulness descends as
senses are stirred

A soft plop followed by gentle
padding movements along a
feathered coverlet

The familiar, musty, cobweb smell filtering
into the nostrils

A steady repetitious hum drawing to a
crescendo
as it nears the eardrum

The sudden tickle of a nose being touched with
whisper-soft fluff

Eyes snapping open as a
weight
drops
suddenly on my chest.

The morning ritual—
my cat wake-up—
has repeated itself.

—Kay Tate

November 23, 1988

*And I put on my old blue jeans
and faded pink sweatshirt and dirty sneaks and
dragged the hose out from its garage corner
because the late November day had brought summer back—
a chance for me to wash the windows before Snow
and my hand was on the faucet when you called,
"Mom, are you coming upstairs soon?" and
I thought NO, I'm Going To Wash The Windows.
But I put down the hose and thought
Yes. I will go up now. I'M COMING.
My feet took me up the steps to the kitchen where
you sat with your guitar and I looked at your
sleepy, smiling green eyes as you said LISTEN.
And you began to play.
"I'm rough. Let me start again," you said.
Your fingers moved faster and the music
began to shine out from your guitar
and you hummed
then stopped for a moment and I thought
OH NO! PLAY SOME MORE!*

*Suddenly I remembered:
December long ago in the nursing home.
My dad and mom had come to visit my beautiful grandmother
in her room in that place
And my father asked, "Would you like me to sing for you?"
Light sprang into my grandmother's beautiful, old face
"Oh, yes!"
So we went to the lounge where there was a piano
My mother played and my father sang and
My grandma's eyes never left my father's face.
Other aged listeners drifted in, and nurses,
But my grandmother did not see them:
Her son was singing for her
He stopped
she clapped
"More! More!" she called.
Again he sang, his strong bass voice
Soaring into every corner of the room
"More! More!"
Each time he stopped my grandmother would call,
her lovely face wreathed in smiles
And he sang and sang and sang
And I wept*

*And today you played and hummed for me, just for me,
And did not see the tears of exquisite
Joy and remembering in my eyes.*

        —Joyce Bumgardner

Old man
lying on the sofa
reading romance novels
forgetting them
starting next day in the
same place
picking one up and reading
anywhere
filling the hours
with packaged love
waiting for bedtime

—Vivian Nelson

Purple
when she was six
she carried
her purple pillow
climbed our tall maple tree
to a strong
safe branch
tucked the softness
between two limbs and
sat there on her pillow
in white shirt and sneakers
and her bright red shorts
peering out through
hiding green leaves
like a sweet small bird
sang her lovely
child's song
and gave our hearts
wings
when she was six

—Joyce Bumgardner

Remnants

Worn dairy calendars with pockets
Receipts of the family homestead
in the trousseau trunk
Elegant edges of linen
crocheted by gnarled fingers
McCoy vases with subdued colors
that once displayed meticulous
vibrant arrangements
Toby mugs that captured change
for milk
from Krogh's corner grocery
Antiques
Valuable
Priceless
Remnants of Grandma

—Beth Huntley

Sounds of silence

Walking south down the road
formerly known as
the dirt road just
east of the gravel
now with a sign: Lexington
in the middle of nowhere.
Silence.
No cars, houses or humanity.

A chorus arises:
   crickets sing
   birds call
   leaves rustle
   rocks crunch beneath my feet
   the wind carries the harmony across
   the fields.

Peaceful
Content
Sweet
Not so
silent
after all.

—Terri Moore

The summer you are 80

You are growing old
your skin wrinkled
blue eyes faded
now you wear long sleeves even
in summer
My arms, you say...my arms
for now they show the signs of age
and you always have been proud of your appearance

Beads of moisture slide down your face
for it is hot and steamy
It doesn't matter, I say
It's hot today—wear short sleeves
My arms. I can't. My arms.

In the store a beautiful
flower-sprigged lavender short-sleeved dress
the kind you wore when Dad would say
Isn't your mom beautiful today?
Tucked in soft rustly tissue paper
a fancy gift box I bring it to you
My arms, you say My arms
Never mind, Mom—put it on

You go obediently down the hall
I expect you will return
carrying the box and saying
take it back...my arms

In just seconds you come
dancing lightly over the carpet
twirling round and round
arms flying eyes sparkling
skirts floating the flowers a blur
laughing, breathless,
a little girl in her first wonderful
grown-up dress
and it is your 80th summer and
you are beautiful and I am your proud
mother.

—Joyce Bumgardner

To Charity, the girl with the teddy-bear brown eyes
Go outside and play.
This is no time to study or think or wonder.
Be a child.
Life goes by too fast.
You must conquer rollercoasters
devour bags of candycorn
teach boys to dance.
It takes no courage of you
not to try.
And so much more when you're
Grown-up
to re-live moments
you have never lived before.

—Gabi Kirsch

Too late
Mother is gone now.
So much to do,
So many things to go through.
She was such a saver of things,
Historian, preserver of our heritage.
China cabinets filled with china and silver
passed down from great-grandmother to
grandmother to mother.

The big bureau in the storeroom
Every drawer another page in the history of our family,
White, lacy christening gowns for
Mother and her three brothers,
Little striped breeches and a small
leather baseball cap of my uncle's
Tiny shoes with shiny buttons
instead of laces,
Crocheted dress I recognize from a
photograph of my parents' wedding,
Postcards to my grandfather from
his sister homesteading in Montana
Letters written by Mother to her girlfriend
Sounding like any teenage girl today
About boys and cars, birthday
parties and sleepovers.
Oh why couldn't I
have discovered these things earlier?
Too late to hear the stories
behind each memento.   —Susan Thoms

Wise counsel and cherry tobacco
that sweet scent
of cherry tobacco
always brings you back
pipe cradled in your strong hand

I see you gazing into space
thinking
contemplating
holding your pipe
for that was your way

how wise you were
how dear

(once
months after you died
I followed cherry tobacco all the way through
the supermarket
looking for your face
your voice
the wisdom that went with cherry tobacco
but when I found him he
wasn't
you)

when you died
and our crying was done
we looked at one another
asking
where will we find wisdom now?
and wept again for loss
of the sweet
wise scent of
you

—Joyce Bumgardner

Women's work
running, skipping
up gravel farm roads
gathering wild roses
breathing innocent country air
my cousin and me

There stood the rickety old farmhouse
"No one lives there anymore,"
she said. "Let's go in."

Books spilling
from old suitcases
onto yellowed linoleum floors
clothes in piles
on unsheeted beds
dishes sprawled
on dirty counters
half-empty food boxes
in gaping cupboards

We talked and sang as we
worked—two little girls doing
what women do—

And left wild roses in a
Mason jar on the kitchen table
just in case they
ever came back.

—Joyce Bumgardner

STUDENTS' POEMS:
BY CATEGORY

DEATH

My cat
My cat was
chasing his
tail
just yesterday
and today
he's gone
gone forever.

—Kelly Allhiser, grade 5

My friend
My friend has moved
far away to
another time and
another world.
I remember making crafts in her house.
I remember playing in her yard.
My friend has moved far away to
another time and
another world.
She went through hospitals,
through summers, winters,
springs and falls

She went through a lot
with me
She has moved far away to
another time and
another world.

Now I know she is
safe
wherever she is.

—Maggie Slobodzian, grade 4

My uncle
My uncle died
I cried for days
My friends asked
me to play
but I wanted
to stay
in my room.
That night the
clouds cried
with me
and the stars
started to fade until
there was just one star left
I wondered if
that was a star
at all but
my uncle
watching
watching over
me

—Sarah Erickson, grade 5

F A M I L Y   A N D   F R I E N D S

Christmas spirit
is when your parents say it's
time to stop looking at Christmas
lights but you say no

when you're on Santa's lap
and they tell you it's about
time to get
off but you say not yet

when you are pigging out
on Christmas cookies and your
parents say
that's enough but
you say one more

when you get up at
6 A.M. to
open Christmas presents
and your parents say
sleep until 8 A.M.
but you look in your
stocking
anyway.

—Megan Maguire, grade 5

Crying
My baby sister is
crying
she is very hungry
in the night
I hear her
crying
in the darkness.

She is back asleep now
I don't need to
worry
she is fine
now.

—Stacy Meincke, grade 6

Divorce
It's hard when your
parents get
divorced
I know how it
feels it feels
as if you have to
choose
between them
even though you don't

It is like you were
split apart

You wonder who do you
love more when you
really
love them both
the same.

—Sarah Rubin, grade 5

Jealous
My sister was born
two months
ago
my birthday is in
two days
Mom hasn't asked me
about it
maybe she forgot
I
open the
door to go
inside...
SURPRISE!

—Katey Honsey, grade 5

Memories
*I get memories
from my mom.
My uncle died before
I was born.
I get memories
from my mom.
She tells me things she
remembers about
him.
I get memories
from my mom.
She tells me sad times
she tells me happy times.
I get memories
from my mom.
Like the times when
her family
all went swimming together
at the lake when she was
little.
I get memories
from my mom
and I love it.*

—Brigette Robbins Peterson, grade 3

My little sister
*She needs to know
everything
listen to each
conversation
use my sweater
She's sometimes weird
and I am like her.*

—Karin Cohen, grade 4

One night
One night
with the clouds
rumbling
and the flowers
dying
and the trees
praying
I thought of your
pleasant, sweet, smiling
face
Wishing you were here so
I could
touch it
hold it
and bless it.

—Lori Mogard, grade 6, *Prairie Winds*

Small town talk
Small town talk
is when there is not much to
talk about
nothing is
going on besides
small town
talk.

—Brant Rinehardt, grade 6

Swimming pool
A pool is cool
and nice but
it's not fun without your
friend
your friend who plays around
in the pool with you.

But if your friend moves away
what fun
will the pool be?
You could play with your
brother
or sister
but no one is like your
friend.   —Brianna Anderson, grade 3

F E E L I N G S   A N D   D R E A M S

Alone
When I am home
alone
it is
dark
mom and dad
leave
quickly I go lock the
door
pull the
shades and
sit there
all
alone.

—Deanna Harvey, grade 6

Creaks
Creaks from the
floorboards and
opening and
closing of doors
scares me when I
am alone at night.

When I'm in my
bed I hear more
creaks and I pull
the covers over my
head.
Sounds like a troll or
witch coming in to
scare me and make
me scream then I
hear something go
THUMP
I get up
slowly and turn on the
light.

—Ryan DeRoos, grade 6

Dreams

Good dreams
are light feathery things
dancing things
with soft colors
of a rainbow
and the golden sparkle
of the
sun.
They are soft as a
summer cloud
and they smell of
fresh-baked cookies
right out of the oven.
You cannot look for a dream;
they look for children,
very special children
on whom they spill
journeys and tales
of long ago.

You cannot write about them:
they are too magical
for
black and white.

Whenever you hear
the tinkling sound of
fairy bells
it just might
it just might
be a dream
sweeping your way.

—Sarah Podenski, grade 5

Flying

Fly, fly, I say
don't be afraid
the sky is ours
soaring high
the world below
away from
sadness, fear and
hate
just close your
eyes and
fly   —Anonymous

Gardens

*A garden
is a magical place
it is just like
an indescribable feeling
bubbling up inside me*

*It is wonderful to be
in charge
of something
it feels like
you are growing up
so fast
with every seed you
plant.*

—Tricia Lind, grade 6

Gone!

*In life you lose things that
mean a lot to you—
a toy, a favorite teddy bear,
or even a friend.
When they leave,
you feel like an empty
lemonade glass
on a hot summer day
like a piece of you
is missing.
But there is nothing you can
do about it—
once they leave, they're
gone.*

—Lucas Holter, grade 6

Happiness

Happiness, oh happiness,
How do you come
through my anger?

Happiness, oh, happiness,
How are you
always there?

Oh child, oh child,
I come through anger because
you call me.

Oh child, oh child
I'm always there because
I'm part of you.

—Elyse Tadich, grade 3

Hurting

I'm hurting inside
feeling like a helpless fawn.
What is the meaning for my life?
Why was I put here?
I'm unsure which direction to go.
Who will guide me?
Will I ever find someone?

The doe finds its fawn,
but
when will someone
find me?

—Sara Wencl, grade 7

I can
I can fly on wings
made of dreams
or I can dance on
newfallen snow.

I can explore
the depths of the sea
or race with the
wild north wind.

I can sail
through the
stars
or explore the
deepest dark caves.

And I can soar as
high as
I want
if I let my
heart
have wings.

—Carissa Nelson, grade 7

Imagination
I love the way birds
soar
in the sky
dogs
walk on the ocean sand
flap their ears and
fly
if dogs don't need wings I
don't
fish fly, dogs fly, birds fly
maybe
I can
fly

Cats fly
wind up their
tails
and up they
go—
And
I will fly too!   —Heather Walter, grade 4

In the mold

In the mold
is what you're supposed to be
how you're supposed to act
and
think.
They say
in order to be successful
you need to
fit the mold
Not me!
I will never
fit the mold
I don't want to.
I just want to be
me.

—Sarah Whebbe, grade 6

Moving

Why do we have to move?
Can't we just stay here?
Leaving friends behind
all the packing, loading, lifting
is it really worth it
sad times for everyone
I will make new friends
but I will never forget the
ones I leave behind.

—Christina Omdahl, grade 6

Music
Gentle
Peaceful
Wonderful music
brings me to
another world
I ride a unicorn
across a meadow
or
a war horse out to find a
dragon guarding hidden
treasures

Music
Gentle
Peaceful
Wonderful music.

—Sarah Erickson, grade 6

My grandpa
Grandpas are
nice. My
Grandpa Herb
lives up
north. He
had a
stroke about
a year ago. Now
people
have to
help
him.
Strokes
are scary.
Grandpas
are nice.

—Brian Terhaar, grade 4

My own home

I have a longing for
freedom,
a thirst for escape,
a place to be myself.
I want to create,
create something so
beautiful that only I
can see the beauty
within it.
I want to go someplace,
someplace I don't have to talk
to anyone or anything,
just be myself, a place
to get away from my
troubles. I want my own
place I can call
HOME.

—Lindsey Jo Hatz, grade 5

My place

I have an imaginary place
only I know about.
Nobody bothers me.
Nobody plays with me.
Sometimes I get lonely
then
I think of all the
unicorns
and friends I have
with me

but sometimes
I need
somebody
real.

—Cassie Cunningham, grade 6

My shoes

Do you know
what it is like to
be in my
shoes?
People always
screaming and
shouting
at you
being mean to you
telling you off?
What I want to say is
Go away!

—Shaina Zuppke, grade 3

Odd

Being one in a million,
Wearing two different shoes
Like an inner tube in the
middle of a lake,
Being the only one with glasses,
Standing out and not being able to
change it,

Having your hair not brushed,
Not having any friends,
Having lots of torn
and scribbled-on things,
Being the only one with marks
All over your hands,
Being different from everyone—
It's like going fishing and getting a
shirt
instead of a
fish.

—Kelly Westlund, grade 6

Perfect

She is so
perfect
and I seem like
nothing.

When we're together alone
everything is just fine
but when someone else is around
she transforms into a
boasting
beast
That's when I fill with
anger, jealousy and tears
That is when she is
Everything
and I am
Nothing.

—Lindsay Lueders, grade 5

Pictures

See the beautiful
pictures
see them
flying
on the wall
like airplanes
in the blue
masters of art
paints of different
shades
high and flying
different
shapes and sizes
all in one
frame

—John Torgeson, grade 5

Secrets
When you left me
I had a
secret

If you had
stayed
maybe
you could have
heard my
secret

It was that I
loved you.

—Katie Ulwelling, grade 7

Sharing my poetry
Oh, no!
Oh, no!
I'm up next
What will I do
My stomach is
in a bag
My eyes are
bulging out
All my teeth
are gone
My fingers and toes
are curled up tight
Now I can't even
Hold
  my
   paper

—Anonymous

The sky

The sky is
high blue and
endless
the clouds hide
wonderful sights
soaring
flying
searching for something
something beautiful
something
mystical

I wish I could fly.

—Jenny Goodwill, grade 6

The sound of rain

At night when it rains
I feel safe
        I go to a far away place
            And dream.

Pitter patter,
hear the rain
but in a far away place
I dream.

In the morning
Plants have dew-drops and
the look of spring
but

at night when it rains
I feel safe
I go to a far away place
And dream.

—Amanda Dalquist, grade 3

Swimming
I like to swim
on a nice
hot day
it makes me
calm down.

I like to swim to
get the anger
out of me
and when it's gone
I don't want to
get out.

Some days I feel
like I live there.

—Heather Hadenfeldt, grade 4

F U N   A N D   P L A Y

Behind the old wrinkled face

Behind the old, wrinkled face
and withered hands
there is YOUTH.
If they were in shape
they would do what
any young would do—
roll down hills,
climb trees,
jump down into piles of straw
Maybe they do that
when we're not around.

—Nicole Mari Oetjen, grade 6

The bumps

Steep
giant bumps everywhere
ouch
you hit one and fall
flying from side to side
hitting so hard
knees wobbling
keep steady
skis like rockets
faster
bang
you fall again
boom, boom
hitting the moguls hard
flying off a jump
crack!
ski breaks
fall on your face
bruised up
do it again
carefully.

—Connor Toole, grade 6

Buzzbait
Cast onto the water
under the sycamore tree

Begin your retrieve
watch the bubbles behind

Then the explosion comes
the lake surges with
waves from the bass that
killed your
buzzbait.

—Tom Hazelton, grade 6

California
warm sunshine
I can feel it on my face
seeping into my skin
making me warm
all over
cool sometimes
rain—the beach is deserted
everybody's dripping wet
ducking into little seaside shops
friendly people
"weather's beautiful"
tan lifeguards
grouches shaking sandy towels
in my face
small towns
big cities
visalia
los angeles
disneyland
families
children crying
dropping ice cream cones
laughing
having fun
California
wish you were here

—Micheie Luhm, grade 6

Camping

Fun is camping
camping with my friend
going fishing,
not catching fish
talking, gossiping in the tent,
bike riding on bumpy trails
over a small rough
bridge
playing pool against my sister and her friend,
not always winning
swimming
swimming in the lake
playing in the sand
making sand castles
CAMPING.

—Judy Miska, grade 6

Cars

Big and
little
fast and
slow
running
up and
down
the
freeway
like millions
of running
ants

—Anonymous

The cave

When I call
in the cave
it
calls back
I think there's
something
at the
other end.

—Cooper Warne, grade 4

The dark night
I like the night
it's so dark and cool
My friends and I play ditch at night
for hours until we have to go in.

I like the dark.
You can't see anything.
We play hide and go seek
I always wear black and no one
can ever find me
even if I'm in an easy spot.

I laugh when they give up on me
because they walked
right past me.

That's why
I like the dark night
because I play in it
with my friends.

—Valerie Stone, grade 4

Fireflies
As the sun goes to sleep
the night wakes up
Tiny fireflies start to turn on
Children come out with
lights
on their minds
We sit on the damp grass and
wait
Suddenly they arrive
red and blue sparks
We grab our jars
hurry to capture
as many as we can to
show our friends
I catch a green light
My sister catches a red light

When morning begins to rise
we let our lights go
saving our jars for the
next firefly night to come.

—Alaina Oas, grade 7

Footprints
When I used
to live where
I used to live
I used to walk
close to the side
of the lake and
leave
wet
footprints.

—Anonymous

Hunting
all alone
animals watching you
putting bullets in the gun
shooting the gun
gutting deer
bringing them home
being cold
sitting
walking in the woods
WHAT!
something moved
you look through the scope
YES!
it's a buck
you aim
you look at the deer's face
you point the gun down at the ground
you fire
BANG! BANG!
the deer looks up
you fire again
the deer jumps over the bushes
goes beyond your sight to its family
and you
  feel
 happy.

—Anonymous

Hunting
hunting
is the
owl
listening to the
mice scurrying below

hunting
is the
fox
tracking the
snowywhite rabbit

hunting
is the
kingfisher
searching the
lake

hunting
is the
man
sitting in the
tree
watching the
deer.

—Jay Harrison, grade 4

I don't like cleaning!
I want to go high in the air
in a hot air balloon.
I wanna get away from the loud noise.
I don't wanna have to scrub the bathroom.
I wanna soar in the sky like a
bird flying
I just don't wanna clean the house.

—Missy Schlichting, grade 5

Imagine this

Imagine this
An animal with an
elephant's head, a
giraffe's neck, a
lion's body and
mouse feet.
Imagine that for a
change.

—Steven McMahon, grade 4

Kitten

The kitten looks
like a
furball
that has just been
washed
and
blow-dried.

—Jessica Petrich, grade 6

My dog

I think FUNNY is my dog,
Her big brown eyes searching for
plastic to
* grab*
away from us.
When supper comes she

scans the table for some
scraps of food.
As she sits on the stairs
I wonder if she knows I
saw her
take that cookie.

—Maggie Slobodzian, grade 4

My little sister
My little
sister's best friend
comes over,
they play horses
they say this
horse is this
horse's boyfriend they
also play
barbies

the
barbies
get married on
horses
the barbies
also climb trees
I don't know much more
than this 'cause whenever
I come into the room they hit
me on the head with the
barbies and the
horses

—Ross Hopeman, grade 5

My yo-yo
Up and down 2X

That's all it
ever
does
Up and down 2X

—John Nelson, grade 3

On the frontier

tap tap tap
went the
hooves
of the
horses
and the
cowboys
dancing
with their
gals

everyone's
cheering
clapping
laughing
around the
gleaming campfire

When nightfall comes
it is
quiet.

—Jolene Bucher, **grade 5**

Painting

The clean
sheet of
paper
the many colors
to choose from
the silk
black
paintbrush
the beautiful
painting

—Katie Hagen, **grade 3**

Right here
Cold water
I am relaxed,
floating as the wind blows,
nothing on my mind—
all my thoughts leave,
just floating in cold
ocean water,
feeling the warm sun
shining on my body
no noise
just the waves
I don't want to be anywhere else.

—Melissa Nicholson, grade 6

Soccer
The ball rolls
silently
across the
newly
cut grass
I hear my heart
pounding
in my
ears
I turn to face the
goalie
my leg swings
back
then
forward
the goalie
lunges...
my coach
yells
with
JOY.

—Nils Lundblad, grade 3

Stars

Stars
I'm under the stars
stars
All alone just reading under the
stars
stars
Mom leave me alone
Stars

—Melissa Flaten, grade 5

Troll

I was the Troll
mean evil and rotten.
I was to stand guard
against my enemy.

My sisters were the good guys
who tried to take my stuffed animals.
But if I caught them,
I could have them for lunch.

I would always be the bad guy
because I was the smallest.
I always had the most fun,
because I made the rules.

—Justin Reichert, grade 9, *Prairie Winds*

WAR, PEACE, FREEDOM

American flag
It's so pretty
waving in the air
and when you see the stars
it makes you want to get right up
there and
ride it.
The red and white looks so beautiful
but then
we do have all these
wars.

—Anonymous

Birds
Birds are free to do
what they want.
They are like people
except without boundaries.

They are like people when they
are captured—
then birds are not free.
They can't have fun any more.

People have boundaries
People are not
free.

—Kelly Thomason, grade 6

Freedom

*Freedom is
birds flying
people singing
fish swimming
happy thoughts running free.
Freedom is
writing poems
in control
no rules
vast
open
happiness bouncing everywhere—
Freedom!*

—Katy Micka, grade 6

Peace

*You have to have surgery
before you have peace*

*You have to have death
before you have life*

*You must have a dream
before reality comes*

For one makes the other

*Surgery on the soul
removes tumors of
hate*

*death of prejudice
is what gives you Life*

Dreams are what help you

*Meet your ideals
and all these things I
will give you
Peace*

—Meredith Reiches, grade 6

Peace

Peace is more than
no war.
Sometimes we forget that
peace is present
when we are happy
and when we are loved.
Even in times of sorrow
and silence
peace is there.

Peace can be a soft wind
or a light rain
peace can be
the whole world together
in harmony
with caring and
a warm smile.

Peace is never
hatred
prejudice
loneliness.

It is respect
for this world
and for all people,
and peace
endures.

—Kjersten Ellingston, grade 8

A ray of life
at the site of the bomb
desolate houses
insides exposed to the cruel world
whole walls caved in
remains of gardens
flowers crushed
empty doorframes,
doors hanging from a single hinge
but...
a lone chimney
standing proud
independent, with no house
to hang on to
sweet bird chirps fill
the air
from high above
atop the chimney,
pink beaked heads straining up
for food

despite everything
...the dark clouds
...the raging storm,
a ray of shimmering light
shines through the
darkness,
a tiny
but gigantic sign
a sign of hope,
a sign of peace.

—Tasha Baron, grade 7

Starving child
Starving child
small and
hungry
come with me
I'll help you
I'll make you
strong
so you can
stop hunger
with me
some day

—Maggie Monahan, grade 4

Watching
What is this thing spreading
throughout the world
flowing everywhere like
spilt milk?
I follow it
watching what it's
doing
It's changing people,
I know.
The deep hollowness I saw
has gone away.

What is this thing spreading
throughout the world
I see people being
kind and friendly,
helping each other.

What is this thing I see?
I see peace.

—Liza Hicken, grade 8

T H E   W O R L D

Clouds
The sky like a brilliant blue easel
sprayed with dazzling white paint
clouds that swirl and turn with the wind
casting shadows to cool you
in the hot summer sun
clouds bringing rain and snow
so big and happy
smiling down at you.

—Christina Omdahl, grade 6

Countryside
At the crack of
dawn
the countryside's at its
best
with shimmering golds, yellows,
oranges
shining on the ripening
wheat fields
the golden sun speaks a word
of hello with its bright shine
and the wheat waves back
as the wind blows through it
that's what I love about the
countryside.

—Patti Meyer, grade 6

Deep in a forest

Deep in a forest down by the pond
a butterfly flies, a lion yawns.
Fish are jumping,
animals drinking
down by the pond.

Deep in a forest, in a cave
a bear cub awakes
with a big yawn and shake.
He wakes with the morning light
in the cave.

Deep in a forest,
down by the hillside,
deer are hiding, animals running—
the hunters are coming,
Down by the hillside.

Deep in a forest
that is now nothing,
Is dirt and sand;
for we caused the problem—
we ruined the animals' homes
Down in the pond,
Deep in the cave,
Down by the hillside,
Deep in the forest.

—Alisha McHone, grade 5

A deer

Whisking through darkness like an owl,
Soft, fuzzy fur falling from a thicket of thornbushes
He dashes, leaps, glides over fences
Waiting in the forest for a crack of thunder,
He catches the air and dashes into the night,
once again, for shelter.

—Betty Spider, grade 9, *Prairie Winds*

Flooded river

A flooded river:
Twisting like a snake.
Swallowing up the banks.
Mean as a dinosaur,
Eating up roads, sheds and bridges.
Destroying everything in sight.

—Andrew Gjovik, grade 5

Frost

Misting speckles of
hiding adventure,
mysterious excitement waiting
to jump out at you.

Covering the window
with a safe protector,
curious shapes,
interesting forms of
coziness.

Sunshine,
melting you to a
puddle
on my windowsill.

—Hannah Lund, grade 4

Haircut

Hair
all over the
floor
talking
ladies under the
dryers
coffee cups in their
hands
it's what I see
every time I
get my
hair cut

—Jamie Pulkrabek, grade 5

I am going away
over the field
through the dew
I am going away
to a gurgling brook
I am going
home.

—*Denise Tesmer, grade 5*

The meadow
I'm running through the meadow
the warm sun and the
strong breeze brushing my face
I inhale the deep fragrance
of springtime flowers.

I'm a bird soaring through the
open sky
no worries in my head
I sit down in waving green grass and
let the sun warm me like a
toasted marshmallow
I tingle with excitement—
This is a day to remember.

—Gina Engesath, grade 6

Nature

I love nature
it's a wonderful sight
all the animals and trees living together
FREE!

When hunting season arrives
that means flight—
some die, others live
to struggle
Guns go off, slowly down they go,
DEAD!

When axes come out
Some trees stand while
others fall down,
DEAD!

Some animal just lost his home.

—Kim Wiita, grade 6

Night

Night is
like a
blanket
covering
daytime
and making everything
dark.

—Jennifer Oskopp, grade 5

Night
I like
night
after dinner
I get ready for bed
there I stare at
the stars
the milky way
the big and
little dipper
When I see them I
think of a glass of
water
I want to reach
for the big cup and
drink it all

—Anonymous

Night
Stars at night
are like
the
eyes of my cat

The moon
is like
the top
of my favorite tree

Raindrops
on my window
are like
birds
pecking on a glass jar

The night is so
nice.

—Mike Sobocinski, grade 5

O Sun
O Sun, O Sun,
How do you like being
so big and
made of fire?

O Sun, O Sun,
How do you like living
in the sky?

O Girl, O Girl,
I love being fire—
It's my favorite thing.

O Girl, O Girl,
I love the sky—
I can pretend it's
mine.

—Mila Ghose, grade 3

Passing by
Along roads and rivers,
churches, houses and castles,
People, strangers live there.
You will never see them,
Never get to know them.
Just passing by,
a light breeze
not leaving a trace.

—Ute Engel, grade 12, *Prairie Winds*

Perpetual war
The tide
   like a war
     never ending
         two sides
     never victor
  never failure
always torment
      always fury
        never ending war
          forcing the enemy back
      further and further
    again and again
like clockwork every day
    The tide a perpetual war

—Josh Kleeberger, grade 8

Rain
O who is
tapping on my
door
who is
tapping on my
door?

It is me,
me,
the
Rain.

—Dain Olsen, grade 3

Rain party
      Rain
          comes floating
            in a
            party
            of clouds
          filling the sky
with darkness
'til it bursts
out laughing
thunder

Sparklingclear water
races
to the land
            below

All through the rain shower
drops of water dance
on roof tops with the wind,
thunder keeping the beat until
it all moves on
and the party comes to an
end

Then raindrops fall
lazily,
slower, slower
until there are no
more.

—Angela Ellis, grade 5

River
    so strong
       like the
          Wind
             with lots
                of creatures
                   floating
                     floating
                    in
                      you,
                         big ones
                           small ones
                             floating away all
                             for you
                               are with
                                   the
                            Wind!

—Aaron Johnson, grade 6

Soft silent sea
I walk
along the beach
listening to songs the
animals
sing

Spears and nets
make me cry
the soft blue waters
where whales live

Silence please—
the sea is
hurting.

—Jenny Granger, grade 5

Wild horses

The thunder
of their
feet
the high-pitched
neighing
the mane like a
whip
cracking
cracking

When I look
it's too late—
they're gone.

—Jessica Gauger, grade 5

Wind noises

Wind carries noises from
the north, south,
east, west—

It brings gun shots
thunder

It brings singing
birds' music

It brings kids' crying
rain

Wind carries
lonesome noises
and happiness

When people hear the
wind's noises
their
ears
get bigger
and they
run for shelter
or
they listen to
the wind
with
joy

—Jodi Rick, grade 5

Windy tree
Think of the
muscles a
tall tree grows
in its leg
and in its foot
in its widespread
toes
not to tip over and
fall on its
 nose
when the wind
blows or hustles
and tussles!

—Bobby Thompson, grade 4

Winter
Ooh!
The weather
so cold
so white
so winter.

—Rebecca Roper, grade 6

EXAMPLES FROM INSTRUCTIVE SECTION

Bad farmer
Kill the cow and starve the horse!
Crack the eggs and set chickens on fire!
Melt the tractor and burn the crops!
Knock down the sheds and the barn!
Blow up the elevators and bins!
Cover the land with toxic waste!
Start the tree rows on fire!
Do you think I shouldn't be a farmer?

—Andrew Gjovik, grade 6

Broken heart
Sitting here I see
a couple
walking hand in hand,
happy together...
I know them well.
I wish I
could be in
his arms
instead of her but that's
impossible but I can't stop
thinkingthingslike that.

My bubble pops
and I'm back on Earth
free to think those thoughts
in my bubble land but
not here.

—Lacy Marie Jacobson, grade 8

Bubblegum
You can chew 'til it's really
soft
or blow a big, huge bubble
or even share a piece
with someone
and
chew it 'til your teeth hurt
I spit mine out the
car window.

—Krystal Grandson, grade 5

But
but...our society prohibits it, never can it be
first in a sentence, can't be a main idea, always
there, always meaningless

but...means nothing, a boring word say the rules,
it has no rights

but...what is it for (connects two sentences, say the rules)
but...what is its meaning (nothing, say the rules) not in definition
in soul (soul is not in the mechanics of writing, say the rules)

but to me but is freedom in poetry, used first and often.

—Mitch Bullard, grade 8

Butterfly
Butterfly
golden cream
soft fuzz
butter color
tiger stripes
falls to mossy ground
butterfly
golden cream
wings as big as an
apricot.

—Jessi E. Vollmer, grade 6

Call for a star
Stars in the sky
loving stars
happy stars
stars to light the sky
dreamy

when in trouble,
call for a star
he will calm you down
he will help you.

—Lee Craig, grade 6

Canoe trip

The water is calm
the air cool
I am in a canoe
ahead—small rapids
rushing faster faster
the canoe tips over
I'm soaking wet

We come out of the river's mouth
it's wavy I almost tip
again I reach shore
my hands
blistered
I LOVE CAMP!

—Matthew Sager, grade 6

Covers on my bed

Covers on my bed
snuggly
toasty warm on a cold winter night.
Covers on my bed
protection from
the big bad bogeyman.
Covers on my bed
love
as Dad and Mom tuck me in.
Covers on my bed
bright and blue
highways that I run my toys on.
Covers on my bed
the tent
my friend and I play in.
Covers on my bed
what Mom tells me to make
every morning.

—L. Peder Larson, Teacher

Cows and pigs
Cows and pigs
die
while I watch
helplessly
as mean men
shoot them down
in the graying
land
and drop them
from the sky
from the barn
covered with
red

—Jesse Carsten, grade 6

Dear Stone
Dear Stone,
how does it feel to
get run over?
To get thrown
across the yard?
To be slung into the air
by a
slingshot?

Dear Boy,
it feels soft to get
run over by a car.

It feels good to be thrown
across the yard and
see the sky
and it feels neat to get
snapped by the rubber string
it's like I'm
flying!
That's how it feels.

—Anonymous

Death
Death is a
dreadful thing it can happen
to any living thing
My grandmother
died like a snap
like a bullet from
a gun
Now I sing this
song to you
in poetry.

—Rachel Lemon, grade 3

The empty schoolyard
Lonely, empty space
Forgotten bikes waiting for their owners
Blue teeter-totters banging up and down
Blown by a ghostly wind
Silent echoes of children shouting
Left over from the weeks before
Swings with their empty canvas seats
Blowing in the breeze

Will I be this empty when I must leave?

—Eleanor Klostergaard, Teacher

Farming
Cows in the barn are silent.

You hear tractors roaring up
and down the field,
Kids in the pig barn trying to
catch a squealing, screaming
pig,

The smell of new baked rolls
for the farmers,

Dirt crunching under wheels,

Old barns sitting there
unused, sagging by the unused
field,

Fragrant, newly cut hay in the fields

But the farmers take their guns to
the barn and that's when I cover my
ears and eyes
and go crying to my
mom. I'm trying to think of
something else.
Tomorrow I won't find all of them
there. I'll go back to take the garbage to
the burning pit and see all the cows
lying there
dead.

—Jeremy Bursell, grade 6

First day of deer season
*It's my first time
hunting for deer
by myself.*

*So I was sitting in my stand
next to the ash swamp
I hear a noise over my head
it's a squirrel
I try to make it shut up
shake the branch and
it leaves.*

*I had doe scent on the tree
I hear a crashing coming
I'm so nervous I can barely lift
my gun
I see it!
My gun is
shaking in my hands*

*It's sniffing the tree
There it is
A ten-pointer
My first deer I ever got,
First day of season
First time I have hunted alone!
It was so cool*

My brother didn't get anything.

—Richard McCorison, grade 6

For my grandpa
The Old Thresher
enveloped his
silo in the woods
with
space dancing.

—Craig A. Nelson, Teacher

Fun and excitement
I like fun and excitement
I like to go on roller coasters
Screaming
My stomach is tying itself in tiny knots
My hands hold tight on the bar in front of me
Twirling
Twisting
I feel excited
Like I'm going to explode or fall off
Corkscrew
Tunnels
I hear thousands of people screaming
I see them lifting their hands
Sick
Excited
I love this!

—AnnaMaria Sjol, grade 6

Grandpa
My grandpa has Alzheimer's.
He doesn't understand.
It makes me unhappy
but not mad.

But then I think,
MEMORIES.
When Grandpa would put me on his lap
sing Ride a Cock Horse
and bounce me up and down
I would listen to his funny jokes
with his twinkle in his eye,
smell the aroma of Grandma's cooking
Grandpa's falling asleep.
Carefully I get off his lap,
quiet not to wake him,
hear his quiet breathing
which gives me no worries, no cares.

Now I look into Grandpa's eyes
Nothing shows he understands
Except the twinkle in his eye.

—Krissen Johnston, grade 6

Happy

When I am happy or
excited I feel like a
balloon with too much air
about to burst

When I am happy
filled with joy
I'm the sun that
brightens the day

When I am happy
feeling good
I'm a blanket to
warm cold feelings

But when I am sad
filled with sorrow
it is a whole different
story.

—Jessica Brannan, grade 6

Lonely

When I'm lonely I feel
like I'm in a
dark place and
no one
cares
I feel water
down my
face
my stomach feels like it's
on a
rollercoaster
I feel like I'm on a
racetrack
racing
to get free to
happiness.

—Brittney Schwager, grade 3

Me
Florida has oranges
California has trees
Wisconsin has dairy—
But Minnesota has me!

—Stephanie Andreson, grade 8

Weird
my dad
is weird and so
is my
family
speedy is fast
but
I'm still not
funny

—Jackie Eckblad, grade 5

My secret place
My secret place is somewhere
but I can't tell you.
My secret place is so secret that
nobody
knows about it.
It is my place
to get away from
everything
and be
alone.
My secret place is
my room.

—Chris Robson, grade 4

The Park Hotel
They sold my life today
The auctioneer raised his gavel and pounded the blow
A hundred years of history lost except for my memories
No more the wide cement porch
where old people rocked and we roller-skated
No more the aging lobby where my brother and I
competed shooting his BB gun
The empty third floor where we were scared
by a ghost
No more put-together rooms of our apartment
I'll never get to curl up and read
in the window seat again
Never look out my bedroom window
to reassure our dogs
Who will climb my willow tree
to strip for Indian gum?
run to catch a ride on a baggage car?
Gone is our ancient bellhops' comforting presence
My mother's lament—But we don't have a house—
was not echoed by us.
Our hotel was our Beloved Home!

—Cindy Karner, Teacher

A peaceful day
Today is a peaceful day with
fish roaming dark waters
lakes of sunlight pouring in the window
deep blue sky where hawks circle
while a small bird builds
its nest of twigs and leaves
rolling waves topping the shores
bees gathering nectar for their hives
flowers bursting with rainbow petals
clouds an ocean of cotton waves
and me
staring at the sky
wondering
if I will ever see a day
like this
again.

—Mike Graff, grade 5

Pop
pop is
cold and
hard in the can
cold so cold
waterdrops
on the side
then whoosh
POP
the can is
opened
all you hear is
fizzfizzfizz
the fizz
of the pop
then gulp gulp gulp
the can is
empty

—Dusty Heise, grade 6

Sadness
Loneliness has cut me
like a knife
even the clouds
seem to
taunt me
It is like a bad dream
Bright colors
seem dull and drab
as I sink into the
depths of despair

My emotions
make me feel like a
patch of muddy snow
on a clear winter morning
and my
imagination
has long ago vanished

The sound of the
piano
down the hall
only seems to give me a
headache
The moon
is covered by
a veil of deep clouds
as I slip into a
restless sleep.

—Emily Mattson, grade 5

The sea   up.
                                                                    surf's
     is   through   you   saying
   sea bouncing   the   and   can   people
The   ground   hear

—Aleea Dugstad, grade 6

Sing

Sing of rain
And butterflies' wings.
Think of everything that
Sings.
Think of the voice
Of the fifth grade choir
As the off-tune notes
Climb higher and higher.
Think of crickets
With whispering wings;
Oh, isn't it peaceful
To think of what sings!

—Meredith Reiches, grade 5

Skateboarding

Skateboarding is
rolling Thunder
coming down a
sidewalk.

—Chase Anderson, grade 6, *Prairie Winds*

Skiing
The thought of
skiing
down a hill
on
two polished fiberglass
skis
sends thrills
through
my body.
Skiing is an
adventure
full of
daring stunts and
breathtaking jumps
that's what
skiing is.

—Brett Hunek, grade 5

Small town
Sitting in my grandpa's old truck
in front of the gas station, watching
old men in overalls going in and out
of the gas station, talking about
farms and tractors, drinking pop
that's almost gone, driving off in
old pick-up trucks, going home to
their farms where the cows need to be
fed and the old tractors are falling apart.

—Jeff Gengler, grade 5, *Prairie Winds*

Spook
Spooky as an owl
scary as a beast
spooky as a maniac screaming in the
night
scary as a backyard grave—
all behind your
closet door!

—Jerry Aure, grade 5

Spring
spring
what a wonderful thing
when puddles lead to
streams of water
and joy bursts
from dull and boring winter
when flowers bloom
and I smell the sweet
fragrance of spring
and everything is
green and lovely
your heart
is overflowing
with joy
and peace
you roll in the grass
with a friend
and dream
a dream that
can
happen
that's why I love
spring.
O
can there be
anything
better than spring
when rain
sprinkles on you
and you dance
and trees grow
and you climb
and reach
the sky!

—Josh Kleeberger, grade 5

Spring fever
Is is robin o'clock?
Is it five after wing?
Is it quarter to leaf?
Is it nearly time for spring?
Is it grass to eleven?
Is it flower to eight?
Is it half-past snowflake?
Do we still have to wait?   —Jake Nieland, grade 6

Stop. Listen.
Stop.
Listen.
Do you hear?
Do you see?
Fighting,
hatred,
prejudice.
Help!
The hurt
the lonely
the hungry
Stop.
Listen.
Just for awhile.

—Erin Adrian, grade 6

Summer
listen to the birds
chirping
watch the roses
bloom
I hear the
ice cream truck—
get some money
quick!

—Katie Hagen, grade 3

These I have loved
The soft looseness of an old cotton sweatshirt
Wet footprints after the first snow
The newborn grass of spring
My birthday cake and Grandma's cookies
A country lane after a spring rain
Listening to a brook gurgling in the night
Faded jeans and love notes
Cool water that soothes a sore throat

I love the softness of an old pillow
Running in the crisp, clean morning air
The smell of freshly baked bread
Listening to people talk
The touch of baby kittens
Getting a tan
Brand new uniforms and Nike shoes
The scares on Halloween
And dusk on cold January nights

I love the thrill of the hunt
Quick glances looking for the prize
Swimming pools, shorts and bikes
Fresh cooked food on winter holidays
Crystals of white snow blowing
Visitors and H.B.O.
The smell of freshly cut grass
Cowboys and home

Or how about extra-spicy, extra-cheesy pizza
Money that never comes to an end
The northern lights on the Fourth of July
The smell of freshly picked strawberries
The sun smiling down on my fishing rod

All these I have loved.

—Group poem from *Prairie Winds*, Rapid City, South Dakota

The summer he left me
My friend and I were friends forever until
he left.
I was happy all my summers but one.
I remember hiding from people
in the big dipper on my
8-shaped block.
I remember the smell of summer that
wasn't even a smell.

I remember the sound of summer that
wasn't even a sound.
I remember when we used to talk about
what we were going to do
the next day.
I remember going to school and talking about
how our sisters are weird.
I remember me sitting alone and
my friend coming to get me out of
boring.
I remember him coming to my house
to play that's when he told me he was
leaving
I was
shattered.
He was leaving our place on
the earth
that was only a speck
on the
map.

—Sean Molin, grade 5

To winter
Leave!
Go away!
I'm ready for spring!
I want to see flowers
And hear birds sing.
I want to go swimming in the lake.
I want to ride my bike.
I want to go camping and
Listen to the night and
The leaves blow
And sing me to sleep just
Dreaming of snow.

—Katie Powers, grade 3

P O E T R Y   B O O K   S O U R C E   L I S T

Following is a list of some poetry books for you to enjoy. These particular books overflow the poetry corner of my own bookcase. There are many, many more. Search your library shelves for poetry you like, go to your local bookstore and find books of poetry to take home, peruse the shelves in "used-book stores" for old goodies, and keep your ears "tuned" for poetry that speaks to you. National Public Radio presents wonderful programs of poetry and interviews with poets—and Garrison Keillor regularly reads poems guaranteed to get your attention. This is just a beginning; please go on to find and add your own favorites.

As Far As I Can See: Contemporary Writing of the Middle Plains, Edited by Charles Woodard (Windflower Press, Box 82213, Lincoln, NE 68501).

Boxelder Bug Variations, Bill Holm (Milkweed Editions, 1985).

A Celebration of Bees (Henry Holt, 1995) and *Cold Stars and Fireflies*, (Harper & Row, 1984) and other books by Barbara Juster Esbenson

The Color of Mesabi Bones, John Caddy (Milkweed Editions, 1989).

The Dragons are Singing Tonight, Jack Prelutsky.

How to Read and Write Poems, Margaret Ryan (Franklin Watts, 1991).

I am Phoenix: Poems for Two Voices (Harper & Row, 1985) and other books by Paul Fleischman.

I'll Meet You at the Cucumbers, Lilian Moore (Macmillan, 1988).

Kicking the Leaves, Donald Hall.

Letters to a Young Poet, Rainer M. Rilke.

Miracles: Poems by Children of the English-speaking World, Edited by Richard Lewis (Simon & Schuster, 1966).

One World at a Time (University of Pittsburgh Press, 1980) and *Weather Central* (University of Pittsburgh Press, 1994) and others by Ted Kooser.

On Poets and Others, Octavio Paz (Arcade Publishing, 1986).
Passwords, William Stafford (HarperCollins, 1991).

Piping Down the Valleys Wild, Nancy Larrick (Bantam Doubleday, 1968).

The Place My Words Are Looking For, Selected by Paul Janeczko (Simon & Schuster, 1990).

A Poetry Handbook, Mary Oliver (Harcourt, Brace & Company, 1994).

The Poetry of Robert Frost, Edited by Edward Lathem (Holt, Rinehart, Winston).

Prairie Winds (South Dakota's young writers' magazine, published twice yearly) Kathy Huse Inman, Editor, 208 E. Colorado Blvd. Spearfish, SD 57783.

Reach for the Moon, Samantha Abeel (Pfeifer-Hamilton, 1993-1994).

Reflections on a Gift of Watermelon Pickle...and other modern verse, Dunning, Leuders, Smith (Scholastic, 1966). Look for this one in used-book stores!

Rose, Where Did You Get That Red? Kenneth Koch (Random House, 1973).

Selected Poems of Langston Hughes (Vintage Books, 1987).

Small Poems Again, Valerie Worth (Farrar, Straus & Giroux, 1986).

Something Permanent, Cynthia Rylant (Harcourt, Brace, 1994).

Spin a Soft Black Song, Nikki Giovanni (Hill & Wang, 1985).

Stars Above Stars Below, Margaret Hasse (New Rivers Press, 1984).

Three Times Three, Phyllis McGinley (Viking Press, 1961). Another one to look for in used-book stores!

Vintage Book of Contemporary American Poetry, Edited by J.D. McClatchy, (Vintage Books, 1990).

Writing Poems, Robert Wallace (Harper Collins 1991).